SUNSHINE *for the* SUNSET

A COMPLETE RETIREMENT PLANNING GUIDE

DR. SANJAY MITTAL

BlueRose ONE.com
Stories Matter
NewDelhi • London

BLUEROSE PUBLISHERS
India | U.K.

For permissions requests or inquiries regarding this publication, please contact:

BLUEROSE PUBLISHERS
www.BlueRoseONE.com
info@bluerosepublishers.com
+91 8882 898 898
+4407342408967

ISBN: 978-93-6261-522-0

Cover design: Shivam
Typesetting: Namrata Saini

First Edition: June 2024

Contents

Dedicated to

This book is dedicated with love to the memory of my father, the late Sh. Inderjeet Mittal ji. He was an esteemed and seasoned banker with the State Bank of Patiala.

This book is not just a collection of words on paper; it's a testament to the values, wisdom, and love you've instilled in me over the years. Since the earliest days of my life, you've been my guiding light, teaching me the importance of curiosity, perseverance, and kindness. I always remember your golden words, "Always save for your rainy days." This quote has always inspired me for savings and planning.

Your unwavering support and encouragement have given me the courage to pursue my dreams, even though the path seemed daunting. With every page I've written, I've felt your presence, urging me forward and cheering me on.

So, Daddy, this book is as much yours as it is mine. Thank you for being my inspiration, my rock, and my biggest fan. I dedicate these words to you with all my love and gratitude.

With great admiration and affection, I am sending this book for publication.

Preface

The majority of people create plans for typical life objectives like purchasing a home, funding their children's college education and marriage, purchasing a high-end vehicle, etc., but they rarely create retirement plans. The majority of Indians think that their kids will take care of them when they retire.

We've all probably noticed that retirees face a lot of difficulties because their children have moved to distant cities or outside of India, leaving them alone and without anyone else to care for them. The acceptance of the molecular family idea is causing a daily shift in how we view our children. Everyone is undoubtedly forced to consider themselves and their post-retirement needs due to uncertainty and insecurity.

One must recognize the value of money in life and the difficulties that come with not saving for retirement, particularly for middle-class individuals who will find it difficult to support their basic needs for Roti, Kapda, and Makaan after retirement.

Early on in life, you should start making planned investments for your retirement. Instead of waiting until tomorrow, you ought to begin saving right now. Due to increasing inflation and a declining value of the rupee, you might not be able to build the corpus you want for your later years. As soon as you begin earning money, you should begin investing so that you can maximize the compounding effect of your interest income (we will go over the power of compounding, which is the eighth wonder, in our chapter on this subject).

To begin retirement planning, you must perform a thorough calculation to determine how much corpus you will need to cover your daily and monthly expenses after retirement. You should review your current spending as it rises annually, factoring in inflation and the depreciation of the rupee. It is recommended that you seek the help of a financial planner or a chartered wealth manager if you lack sufficient financial literacy. They are in a better position to help you plan and check your retirement corpus and learn how to build one.

If you want to build your corpus through traditional assets like bank fixed deposits, PPF, EPF , investments in gold and silver, etc., these may not be sufficient to build the required corpus. On the other hand, if you want to build your retirement corpus entirely through equity and the stock market, that may also not be the best course of action. You need to make plans to build your retirement corpus in a diversified manner using a variety of investment vehicles. Throughout the accumulation stage, a diversified portfolio should be kept in place to reduce investment risk.

We will also learn about financial planning and its significance in this book. The necessity of financial planning and why the average person and retail investors should care about it. Additionally, the value of financial literacy and how to become financially literate will be covered.

We will also gain knowledge about the significance, necessity, and advantages of wills and nomination facilities. We will study choosing insurance plans, figuring out the worth of a person's life, getting health insurance, and setting up an emergency fund.

This book's main goal is to assist readers in making retirement plans so they can live prosperous and healthy retirements as their second innings, independent of others. Given the extremely low level of social security and the rapidly rising cost of healthcare, it is important to understand how much is needed and how to get it.

I have no doubt that this book will assist you in becoming familiar with financial jargon, gaining the fundamental and necessary knowledge, overcoming all financial challenges in your life, and getting ready for your second act.

Your insightful comments and suggestions can be sent to shsanjay.mittal@gmail.com. I can use this to help me improvise for my upcoming publications on various aspects of health and wealth.

Dr. Sanjay Mittal

Introduction

"Retirement" is one of the most certain events in the lives of working personnel, and it is an indisputable fact that we are unable to work indefinitely. We all have to bid our working lives farewell at some point. In India, the retirement age for public sector, semi-public sector, government, and private sector employees is set at roughly 58 to 60 years You are unable to work past a specific age, even if you are self-employed. It is crucial that you start making plans for your retirement years in advance. It is a fact, though, that we often neglect to make retirement plans, particularly when we are younger. We don't worry about our retired lives or how we're going to handle our financial needs until retirement draws nearer.

People are living longer, thanks to medical facility advancements, which means they will need more money to maintain their lifestyle since they will be living long after retirement. Therefore, keep the following suggestions in mind as you prepare for retirement:

1) Make sure you have enough money saved up for emergencies, medical bills, and monthly household expenses after retirement.

2) Enough money is on hand to guarantee financial independence for the duration of your life.

3) Retirement planning needs to be done early because you might not have the zeal and energy to work for a long time or after a certain age to meet your financial requirements.

4) To assist you in realizing your goals and desires, such as taking the vacation of your dreams or continuing your present way of life without making any sacrifices.

Retirement planning should involve figuring out time horizons, projecting costs, figuring out required post-tax returns, evaluating risk tolerance, and creating an estate plan. Initiate your retirement planning as soon as possible to capitalize on compound interest. As retirement plans change over time, portfolios should be adjusted, and financial plans should be updated as necessary.

With the adoption of the nuclear family system, people are now more responsible than ever for retirement planning. Therefore, we cannot rely on our offspring for our later years. Planning for retirement early is essential for achieving a sustainable financial goal. You can achieve all of your financial goals when you have an updated financial plan in place.

The most important aspect of retirement planning is figuring out the right retirement corpus amount while accounting for inflation. For example, in 2010 a liter of same milk used to cost Rs. 25, but in 2022 it will cost Rs. 50. Even though it's common knowledge that milk has become more expensive, the value of your rupee has decreased by 50% during that time. You will therefore only be able to purchase half a liter of milk for the same amount of Rs. 25/-. To clarify, let's say your current monthly expenses come to Rs. 20,000 and you intend to retire in 30 years. Assuming inflation of 6% per year, you will need about Rs. 120,000 per month to maintain the same standard of living. By the time you reach 80 years old, you will need about Rs. 400,000. The retirement amount needed to maintain the same standard of living, when taking the current interest rate environment into account, comes to a hefty sum of about Rs. 50 million.

It is advisable to have a basic understanding of financial planning before beginning any retirement planning. It will be very beneficial to have a basic understanding of financial planning and financial literacy when choosing which asset classes to invest in to get the corpus you want for your second innings. As we move through our different sections, we will cover the fundamentals of financial planning as well as the steps involved in retirement planning. We'll talk about investing in different asset classes to get the necessary corpus, as was previously mentioned.

Drawing from my professional background and my engagement with diverse investors and retirees, we will endeavor to ascertain, via a range of choices, the most secure location for your retirement funds while considering potential growth. As previously mentioned, my experience creating financial plans for hundreds of friends informs the investment options suggested, explained, and prioritized below. It also informs my personal choice of asset classes. But you are free to think about them in light of your understanding and priorities.

"As in all Successful Ventures, the foundation of a good Retirement is, Planning" *-by Earl Nightingale*

Why Retirement Planning Is Necessary

A retirement plan is a set of arrangements designed to give you a pension or income when your career or business ends and you are no longer receiving a stable income. When your employment or business ends and you are no longer receiving a consistent income, you must have a retirement plan to support you. One size does not fit all, meaning that a single planning formula cannot be used for every individual because every person has different needs. Determining different goals, such as consistent income and corpus building, is crucial. Retirement planning is crucial, and you should get started as soon as possible because your golden years will arrive before you know it. Additionally, the rising rate of inflation, the nation's love of gold, and the abundance of financial products that banks and other financial institutions offer make retirement planning in India a difficult task.

Retirement is a significant life stage that most of us will eventually go through. Furthermore, since retirement planning requires forethought and unwavering diligence until the day of retirement, it is an essential process that we must start right away. Contrary to popular assumption, though, retirement planning can be completed with fewer concessions if you put in the necessary research, establish a realistic goal with the aid of a solid investment plan, and persevere. You bear equal accountability for the health of yourself and your loved ones. For this reason, you must be aware of every potential source of retirement income as well as the potential consequences if any are lost.

Pension benefits: The most popular benefit that governments give to retired people is a pension. Because of improvements in healthcare, a greater number of retired people are living longer than they did previously, which is placing pressure on the nation's financial system. In the event that the issuing institution fails, pension plans provided by different private institutions might also be impacted. It is even more crucial that you take charge of your retirement plan in light of everything mentioned above.

Risk Capacity: The next crucial and pertinent issue that will cross your mind when you've achieved retirement age and amassed your retirement corpus is: "How should I manage this corpus?" You shouldn't speculate with your money after retirement. This money is your hard-earned savings over a long period of time. When making investment plans, you cannot play around with your retirement funds.Retirement funds should, in the opinion of many financial consultants, be allocated to investments with the lowest potential level of risk. While this is not a bad idea, but in practice, the zero-risk impact of this approach is disastrous. The main cause of this is that everyone overlooks the risk that comes with inflation, which is the largest threat to your financial security. The conventional mindset in India on retirement investing holds that one should not accept even a slight decline in the investment's nominal value, while simultaneously denying the reality that inflation steadily lowers the investment's real worth by 6% annually.

Basis your income needs while you plan to invest your retirement funds , it is advisable to ascertain your level of risk tolerance prior to choosing any financial instruments. Your willingness to take on a certain level of risk in order to accomplish your goals is referred to as your risk appetite. It's a sentence, or set of sentences, that expresses how you feel about taking risks. An investor with a high risk appetite can make more informed decisions. This is crucial because it allows for the evaluation of the effects of investor decisions and guarantees the adoption of a risk-informed agenda.

Unexpected medical costs: Even the most prepared people might be caught off guard by unexpected medical expenses, creating a financial insecurity. Medical costs can quickly rise due to unanticipated injuries, illnesses, or complications, leaving people to deal with both financial strain and health issues. The costs can rise quickly, frequently beyond the amount that insurance plans pay for or completely surprising people without coverage. These costs can range from ER visits to specialist treatments. These costs might cause financial stability to be disrupted and force one to make difficult decisions between paying for essential medical care or piling up mountains of debt. So, unforeseen medical expenses highlight the significance of being financially prepared as well as the necessity of strong healthcare systems that put accessibility and affordability first for everyone. A strong health insurance coverage is an essential defense against the chaos of unforeseen medical emergencies in the unpredictably changing world of health. It acts as a buffer, providing comfort and security of income during unanticipated medical emergencies.

Without this kind of coverage, people run the risk of having to deal with the financial ruin of increasing medical expenses in addition to the physical difficulties of illness or injury.

Life goals and misconception: When compared to other life stage goals like purchasing a home, funding a child's education, or getting married, people frequently neglect to plan for retirement. They think they have enough money because they have investments in gold, silver, commodities, real estate, and other instruments like EPF, and they believe their kids will take care of them. Regarding the former, there is little doubt that their children will take care of them when they retire, but it is unclear if they have evaluated their needs in addition to the income and liabilities of their children. Due to a variety of factors, including a changing lifestyle, longer life expectancy, high rates of inflation, declining rupee value, and many more, it is very difficult to do that.

However, in the latter scenario, it is unclear if the corpus or savings made will be enough to meet their retirement requirements. It's critical to conduct an analytical analysis right away and create a thorough retirement plan that takes into account all relevant factors, including changing lifestyles, longer life expectancies, high rates of inflation, and others.

Low level of social security: It's not easy to live off of Social Security alone. About 12% of men and 15% of women in older Indian populations say that their monthly Social Security check provides almost all of their income. The benefit is insufficient for many households to pay their expenses. Many Indians have little to nothing saved when they reach retirement age. Because of this, the majority or all of their income comes from their Social Security check. Even with an annual cost-of-living adjustment that was larger than usual—roughly 6% on average—the sharp increases in housing and grocery prices have only made financially insecure retirees more anxious about their future and ability to pay their bills. The effects of inflation are beginning to be felt by the public, particularly with regard to daily necessities. Having a retirement plan is crucial because relying solely on social security will not support you in your later years.

Retirement Age and Life Expectancy: Retirement planning and social structures are based on the notion of retirement age, which is closely related to life expectancy. The age at which an individual usually leaves the workforce and starts to rely on a pension or retirement savings for financial assistance is known as retirement age. Governmental regulations, prevailing economic conditions, and social mores—which differ among nations and cultures—often dictate this age. In contrast, life expectancy is the average number of years that a person is projected to live, taking into account lifestyle decisions, socioeconomic factors, and medical breakthroughs. The global increase in life expectancy has made retirement age a crucial factor in guaranteeing financial stability and maintaining social welfare programs. Maintaining a balance between retirement age and life expectancy is a dynamic task that calls for constant adjustment to changing societal demands and demographic developments. Comparing your life expectancy after retirement and evaluating or deciding when you want to retire are both highly fascinating. The general tendency indicates that you will live longer if you retire earlier in life. All people, however, aspire to retire early. Given that you have worked your entire life, it is quite tragic to retire at 66 and pass away at 67. It is important to prepare your retirement so that you can live it on your terms and worry-free about money after you're retired.

Retirement Planning also depends on your Retirement type: The majority of the service class plans to retire at the age determined by their work, which is often 58 or 60 in India. This type of retirement is referred to as "Normal Retirement" since the retiree receives all of their benefits at their designated retirement age. A large number of other members of the in-service class also plan to retire early, using the early retirement or VRS plan option that permits an employee to leave the organization prior to the official retirement age. In general, an employee might anticipate receiving fewer benefits if they choose to exercise this option rather than waiting until they reach the formal retirement age. Few members of the service class also make plans to retire later than the designated age because they haven't accumulated the necessary corpus or because they have unfulfilled obligations, such as their children's ongoing education or marriage, or for any other reason. We call this postponed or delayed retirement.

Important factors in Retirement Planning of Self Employed or Business Class: Benefits like pensions, P.F., and gratuities that are accessible to members of the service class are not available to independent contractors or business owners. Additionally, there is market risk in the firm or profession that they cannot control. Health problems Related issues might always have an impact on the company, revenue, and retirement fund. Professionals and business people should plan their retirement with these factors in mind.

Required corpus for retirement: While planning for retirement , you need to accumulate the appropriate amount of corpus to meet your essential obligations and needs, as well as to generate a steady stream of retirement income to support your post-retirement lifestyle, in order to reach your retirement goals. The 30X rule, which states that your retirement corpus should be at least 30 times your current annual expenses, is an industry standard when it comes to retirement corpus. According to the 30X rule, for instance, if your yearly expenses are Rs 9 lakh and you are 50 years old, you will require 30 times that amount to live comfortably in retirement.

Retirement Planning Process

When should Retirement Planning Start ?:

People may put off retirement planning because they believe it to be excessively difficult. It is therefore necessary to comprehend the retirement planning process and to plan and implement it appropriately. The more time you have left before retiring, the more probable it is that you will reach your objective. So, it is best to act quickly.

Retirement planning is often thought of as a tool for individuals who are getting close to retirement, but it should be emphasized that your chances of reaching your financial objectives increase with the length of time you have available for saving.

If you begin investing and planning early on, retirement planning will work to your benefit. The monthly investment or saving required to build the required corpus will be too smaller, if you start investing at early age as the investment tenure will be long enough and will allow the money to have the magical effect of power of compounding which is known as the eighth wonder of the world.

People frequently plan to retire later in life because, quite obviously, they place a higher priority on the financial security of their family and children than on their own retirement. People typically begin to consider building a retirement corpus in their 40s, but at that point in their lives, they may find it difficult to set aside enough money for investments and may have less extra income, which may not be enough to meet the requirements.

Above all, getting a head start will enable you to reap the rewards of compounding. When earnings increase or financial objectives such as home ownership, child education, etc. are satisfied and extra money is available, people typically begin saving for retirement in their mid- to late-career years. But by starting late, they are deprived of the opportunities that would have been theirs. Making plans as early as possible is essential because it allows your corpus more time to grow. It's a process whereby the money invested and its profits are reinvested to produce more income.

The longer you wait to start saving for retirement, the more time compound interest has to grow your money.

You may guarantee a comfortable and secure future by coordinating your financial resources with your retirement objectives and making well-informed decisions regarding when to retire with prompt planning. You can adopt an aggressive strategy if you begin investing at a young age. Through various market cycles, tactical allocation will also be advantageous to you. An extended duration can mitigate the risks of inflation by offering the opportunity to generate higher returns.

You'll have more time to organize your money. This implies that you will have ample time to temporarily alter the plan in order to achieve any objective or deal with an emergency before retiring. For instance, you would have a ready corpus to draw from in the event of a medical emergency or a job loss, with the intention of replenishing it as soon as the crisis passes.

The best retirement plans should provide capital preservation, steady returns, and financial security—all of which can be attained through asset diversification. Your retirement years will be easier the more you save during your service years. Retirement ought to be stress-free, accompanied by financial stability and independence. It ought to be a relatively carefree stage of life rather than a reaction to changing circumstances. Since retirement planning takes time, it is imperative to begin as soon as possible.

Power of Compounding

The magical power of compounding is something that has remained one of Warren Buffett's central principal investments. "Compound interest is the eighth wonder of the world. He who understands it, earns it ... he who doesn't ... pays it." — .

The ability of an investment to yield returns on both the principal and the interest accrued over time is known as the power of compounding. Compounding is the process of reinvesting the interest you earn on your investment, which allows you to earn interest on interest earned and, over time, significantly increase your investment.

The tenure that determines when interest is paid or credited to your account determines compounding. Therefore, it's critical to understand whether your investment's compounding is done quarterly, half-yearly, or annually. Banks typically pay interest on cumulative direct deposits on a quarterly basis, which results in four compounding events annually. Conversely, interest is compounded twice a year on Government of India Bonds , NSCs , KVPs etc. due to the bi-yearly payment schedule. Let's try to understand this with below example: -

BANK FIXED DEPOSIT	GOI BONDS / NSC / KVP
Amount Invested 10 lac	Amount Invested 10 lac
Rate of Interest 7% p.a.	Rate of Interest 7% p.a.
Interest Frequency -- Quarterly	Interest Frequency – Half yearly
Maturity Rs.14,14,778/-	Maturity Rs.14,02,552/-

With everything remains the same, the difference in maturity amount is due to the period of compounding.

The following is a summary of the parameters that affect compounding power:-

a) Growth option;

b) Time duration;

c) Tax rate; and

d) Compounding rate.

Let us quickly review the essential guidelines to fully utilize compounding power.

A) START EARLY: -

First and foremost, an early start will help you enjoy the benefit of power of compounding. When earnings increase or financial objectives such as home ownership, child education, etc. are satisfied and extra money is available, people typically begin saving for retirement in their mid- to late-career years. But by starting late, they are deprived of the opportunities that would have been theirs.

Commence investing at the earliest opportunity to allow your corpus more time to grow. It's a process whereby the money invested and its profits are reinvested to produce more income. The longer your money has to grow through compound interest, the earlier you start investing for retirement.

B) Discipline: -

Your primary goal of saving for retirement should be approached with discipline.A methodical approach to investing can assist you in meeting your long-term financial requirements. A young person has the ability to invest for 25–30 years and can devote more money to riskier options like equity. He can then gradually transition to low-risk investments that safeguard your capital. Basis Warren Buffet quotation -- "Do not save what is left after spending, but spend what is left after saving."

C) Patience: -

Many of us have lost our hard-earned money by investing in schemes that promised to double our money in four or five years, as most of us desire quick returns. Never forget that compounding is the source of the powerful reap. Annualized Yield is the most accurate method for estimating the true value of your investment over time.

The total interest, dividends, and other income that an investment produces divided by the investment's age or the length of time the investor has held it is the average yield on an investment or portfolio. More specifically, it's the yield, or total income from all investments, divided by the duration of ownership.

Compound interest and other factors, such as tax benefits through the end of the term, are included in the yield on fixed deposits. Here, the computation operates backwards. The annualized effective yield can be obtained by dividing the total return on investment by the number of invested years. This will give you the yield on the interest you will earn from FD.

The bottom line is to use the Power of Compounding to create wealth for you while you sleep by starting early, investing for a longer period of time, exercising discipline in your investments, and having patience.

How much Retirement Corpus you need

Estimating the amount you will need after retirement to maintain your standard of living is the first step in retirement planning. You ought to be aware of the considerations to make when projecting your post-retirement expenses. It's also a good idea to be aware of your current resources. This will provide you with the amount that needs to be filled in order to meet the estimated needs for retirement. It is only with this figure that you can determine how much money should be saved and create investment plans that will guarantee the desired income stream over time.

Selecting the right combination of retirement plan options from the many options that are available in the financial sector is a crucial next step in retirement planning. We'll go over and expound on the best financial instruments and choices.

Calculating Needs for Retirement:

Prior to beginning retirement planning, the most important thing to do is figure out how much income you'll need to support a comfortable lifestyle and some of your post-retirement goals, such as taking a trip or vacation. Every person has an idea in general of the kind of retired life they hope to lead after they retire. One can estimate the amount of income required in retirement by creating a scenario based on their ideal retirement state and the actual circumstances they may encounter.

The resources you will require to meet your post-retirement needs will primarily depend on three factors:

1) **Retirement age:** As discussed above, Retirement plan can be made like at Premature retirement or obtaining VRS before you reach your set age of retirement if you are a service class , Second is you can retire at the set retirement age of 58 or 60 depends on your company norms or the third class is delayed retirement. In the case of businessmen / professional this will depend upon their

business scenario and the health conditions. When you decide the retirement class as said above, then only you will be able to calculate the corpus required after retirement.

2) **Life expectancy:** The exact length of a person's life is impossible to predict. The one certainty that remains is that, on average, our generation will outlive those of previous generations. That suggests that one should make an effort to plan for a minimum of 25 to 30 years in the future. One would be safer if they planned for a longer time period.
3) **Expected monthly expenditure:** The income required each month to support oneself and one's standard of living is the second factor that would determine the quantity of resources required. This can only be obtained by carefully estimating what one's anticipated monthly expenses will be after retirement.

Estimating monthly spending: A person's monthly spending will vary depending on a number of social and economic factors. Preference-based changes will occur, but the fundamental computations won't change.

a) Daily consumption expenses, such as those for groceries, electricity, vegetables, fruits, milk, and so forth.
b) A major factor in determining spending is housing. If you own your home, you must account for maintenance expenses; however, if you rent, you must also account for monthly rent, which includes utilities, electricity, and any necessary maintenance.
c) The largest item on a person's list of expenses is probably medical. Growing older will inevitably result in higher medical expenses. You should primarily account for the regular medications you will need to take for the rest of your life to treat chronic conditions like diabetes, arthritis, high blood pressure, heart problems, etc. Treatment for conditions like infections, seasonal illnesses, etc., that may occur more frequently should be taken into account. When determining the cost of medical care, take hospitalization, nursing care, and physiotherapy expenses into account.
d) The majority of retired people's favorite pastime is travelling, especially when they are on pilgrimages or attending religious events. Despite this, everyone has a variety of hobbies that they

enjoy. The cost of each of these leisure pursuits should be included in monthly expenses.

e) Children of retirees or those nearing retirement may be approaching their senior year of college, may not be settled in their careers, and may still require parental support to meet their basic needs. One will need to account for these costs well in advance, depending on the age of the child and their retirement age.

It is important to remember that the expenses are calculated for a husband and wife when planning the corpus. When planning a corpus, you must account for inflation and the real rate of return. It is important to confirm whether you have employer-sponsored health insurance or medical insurance when making plans for medical expenses.

Investment Planning

The process of determining your financial objectives and developing a plan to meet them is known as investment planning. The process of investment planning begins with evaluating your financial objectives and creating a list of them. It concludes with investments and ongoing portfolio monitoring. To find your ideal asset allocation, it is crucial to specify a timeframe and the level of risk you are willing to accept.

Choosing to invest is a personal decision that is influenced by a number of variables, including age, age bracket, marital status, responsibilities, and monthly income. As a result, each investor's portfolio is unique; for example, the portfolio of a young person will differ from that of a middle-aged person who is responsible for family responsibilities and from that of a person who is at almost retirement age.

Let's examine the steps involved in investment planning:

Step 1: Creating investment goals:

Goals assist us in achieving life's primary objectives, such as maintaining good health and retiring with a sizable nest egg. The money we allocate to investment products, like stocks, bonds, and funds, has structure and purpose when it comes to our investment goals. Setting financial goals and investing go hand in hand with good personal finance habits like budgeting and emergency fund building. This course on smart investing, "Setting Investment Goals," will teach you more.

Having enough money saved for retirement, covering college expenses, or saving for a down payment on a home are among the common investment objectives that many of us have. Estimating the true cost of each goal is the first step towards setting a meaningful target when you set these or other investment goals.

To make it easier to monitor your progress, it may be beneficial to create separate accounts for each primary objective. Since how you save and invest for short-term objectives like a family vacation will probably differ from how you save and invest for medium- or long-term goals like paying for college or funding your retirement, each account will probably hold different investments or savings products.

Step 2: Evaluate your present financial situation

Determining your current financial situation is the next and most crucial stage in the investment planning process. For instance, a worker in the public sector is qualified for specific retirement benefits such as ESI, EPF, etc. Other savings might also apply to other people as well as employees of the formal sector. One can estimate the difference between what one has and what one desires by using these two numbers: estimated needs and available resources.

We would be able to establish a baseline for the corpus amount that must be acquired in order to be available on the date of retirement once the gap has been estimated. Assumptions regarding the rate of inflation, interest income both before and after retirement, the number of years till retirement, and the number of years in retirement would determine the real amount of corpus that would need to be set up.

The amount of money you have to invest needs to be determined to generate the required retirement corpus. The following methods can be used to assess the state of your existing finances:

Examine your spending plan: Make sure you're spending less than you make by taking a look at your monthly income and expenses. A balanced budget indicates sound financial standing.

Examine your debt: Examine your debt, including personal loans and credit card balances.Look through the last few months' credit card and bank account statements to identify any costs you may have overlooked. Make changes to your budget. Examine your spending patterns and think about cutting back on non-essential spending to free up more cash for debt repayment or savings. Include a section for investing and savings when you list the income and expenses that you and your family members incur each month. Reduce your expenses first if you are spending all of your money and never have any left over for savings or investments.

It is imperative to take accessibility of your investments into consideration. Fixed assets like real estate are not the best choice if you might need to quickly cash out on your investment. Instead, you should invest in more liquid assets like stocks or funds for emergencies.

Risk Analysis

Put simply, an investor's risk tolerance refers to the amount of risk they are willing to assume. The level of risk an investor is willing to take on, considering the volatility of investment value, is known as their risk tolerance. Risk tolerance is a crucial factor in investing since it frequently influences the kind and quantity of investments a person makes. An investor's risk tolerance is influenced by their age, financial objectives, and income. An investor's time horizon is one aspect that influences risk tolerance. When investing in higher-risk assets like stocks with a long time horizon, such as stocks, an investor may be able to achieve higher returns. In contrast, cash investments with lower risk might be suitable for short-term financial objectives.

Risk tolerance is influenced by an investor's potential for future earnings as well as the existence of additional assets like a home, pension, Social Security, or inheritance. When an investor has access to other, more reliable sources of funding, they are able to take on more risk with investable assets. Furthermore, because a larger portfolio has a much lower percentage of loss than a smaller portfolio, investors with larger portfolios may be more risk tolerant.

Nonetheless, investment planning may be carried out using an asset allocation tool and based on an individual's life stages and risk tolerance. Let's clarify in more detail:-

Aggressive Tolerance for Risk: -

An aggressive risk tolerance investor is someone who is willing to take on a higher level of risk in their investment portfolio in pursuit of potentially higher returns. **These investors typically have a longer investment horizon** and are comfortable with the volatility that comes with investing in riskier assets such as stocks, emerging markets, or speculative ventures. They may prioritize capital growth over capital preservation and are willing to endure significant fluctuations in the value of their investments in exchange for the possibility of achieving substantial gains over time.

An investor with a high risk tolerance, or one who is aggressive, is prepared to risk his / her money in the hopes of achieving better returns. At this point in your career, you are still a young person with no significant responsibilities (25 to 25 years of age group generally) . You can now allocate 70–75% of your savings to Large cap funds , index funds or stocks. Typically, astute investors possess a keen awareness of the market and recognize the fluctuation of stocks. They employ tactics aimed at attaining returns that surpass average levels. Investing in capital appreciation is more important to them than income or protecting their main investment. Stocks typically make up this investor's asset allocation, with little to no allocation to bonds or cash.

Tolerance for Moderate Risk: -

Investors with moderate risk tolerance typically seek a balance between capital growth and preservation. They are comfortable with a moderate level of risk in their investment portfolios, preferring a mix of assets that offer both growth potential and stability. Such investors often allocate their investments across a diversified portfolio consisting of stocks, bonds, and possibly alternative assets like real estate or commodities. While they understand that some degree of risk is necessary to achieve returns that outpace inflation, they aim to mitigate excessive volatility by diversifying their holdings. Moderate risk tolerance investors prioritize steady, sustainable growth while also considering the importance of preserving capital over the mid long term.

The age at which someone takes on moderate investment risk can vary depending on individual circumstances, financial goals, and personal risk tolerance. However, moderate risk tolerance is often associated with individuals who are in their mid-career or approaching retirement age.

In general, during the early stages of one's career or when just starting to invest, individuals may opt for a more aggressive approach to capitalize on their long investment horizon and ability to recover from potential losses. As they progress in their careers and accumulate wealth, they may transition to a moderate risk tolerance stance, seeking a balance between growth and preservation of capital.

For many people, this transition typically occurs in their 35s to 50s, although there's no one-size-fits-all answer. Factors such as income level, financial obligations, retirement plans, and overall financial stability also play significant roles in determining the appropriate level of risk tolerance at any given age. Consulting with a financial advisor can help individuals assess their risk tolerance and tailor their investment strategy accordingly.

The goal of moderate investors is to increase their wealth while limiting losses. This investor's strategy is sometimes referred to as a "balanced" approach since their objective is to balance opportunities and risks. Typically, moderate investors build a portfolio with a 50/50 or 60/40 split, or a combination of stocks and bonds. This type of investor can choose to invest in Equity oriented Hybrid funds , Dynamic Asset Allocation funds , Aggressive Hybrid funds or Multi Asset Allocation funds.

Low Risk Tolerance: -

A person with a low risk tolerance for investments prefers to reduce the likelihood that they would experience financial loss from their investment portfolio. Generally speaking, investors with low risk tolerance are more conservative and place a higher value on protecting capital than maximizing returns. Even if it means sacrificing some prospective earnings, they favor assets that provide a high level of safety and consistency.

Investments that are appropriate for people with low risk tolerance include in Bank Fixed Deposits , ultra short term or liquid funds , Post Office Monthly Income Scheme , money market funds, government bonds, CDs, and premium corporate bonds. Comparing these assets to riskier investments like stocks or real estate, it is usually believed that they are less volatile and provide more predictable returns.

Lower returns are generally acceptable to investors with limited risk tolerance in exchange for stability and peace of mind, and they frequently place a higher priority on safeguarding their initial investment amount. They might be especially susceptible to changes in the market and would rather stay away from large swings in the value of their investments.

A low-risk tolerance investing strategy is appropriate for people who value money preservation above all else and are uncomfortable with the volatility and unpredictability that come with higher-risk investments. Individuals who are approaching retirement or have already retired often prioritize stability and income generation from their investments to sustain their lifestyle. They may have limited earning capacity and a shorter investment horizon, making them more vulnerable to market downturns. Some people are by nature less risk-takers and prefer the security of assets that yield consistent, predictable returns. They are prepared to accept smaller prospective earnings in exchange for stability and place a higher priority on the security of their major investment amount.

Emergency / Contingency Fund

Because life is unpredictable, you could be caught off guard at any time by unexpected events like unexpected medical costs, a natural disaster, losing your job, or significant company losses. Not preparing ahead of time for such circumstances not only lands you in a sticky situation during those times, but it also throws your plans into a loop when you have to spend money or take on more debt. As a result, making preparations for this kind of scenario is crucial and should be included in all financial plans.

An emergency fund is a savings account specifically set aside to cover unexpected financial emergencies or expenses. It serves as a financial safety net, providing quick access to cash when needed most. Here's why having an emergency fund is crucial:

Financial Security: Because life is unpredictable, unforeseen costs—like emergency medical care, auto repairs, or job loss—can occur at any time. Having an emergency fund guarantees that you will always have enough money to go through difficult times without having to liquidate long-term investments or take on high-interest debt.

Peace of Mind: It helps to know that you have emergency reserves set aside to lessen the worry and anxiety that come with unforeseen financial setbacks. It gives you a sense of stability and assurance that you can overcome financial difficulties.

Avoiding Debt: In order to pay for unforeseen bills, persons without emergency funds may turn to credit cards, personal loans, or pay day loans. These choices frequently have exorbitant fees, interest rates, and long term financial repercussions. Having an emergency fund on hand helps keep debt from mounting during hard times.

Maintaining financial objectives: Setting up an emergency fund enables you to continue working toward your long-term financial objectives, which can include paying for school, saving for retirement, or purchasing a house. It keeps you from taking money out of these savings or changing course when unforeseen costs come up.

Flexibility and Independence: Financial flexibility and independence are made possible by emergency funds, which let you deal with crises without having to forgo other financial objectives or rely on outside help. It offers you the flexibility to choose based on your requirements and situation rather than your means.

In summary, an emergency fund is a vital component of a healthy financial plan, providing stability, security, and peace of mind in the face of unexpected events. Building and maintaining an emergency fund should be a priority for everyone, regardless of their financial situation or income level.

Where to invest your money for Emergency Fund: -

When investing your emergency fund, the primary goal is to prioritize safety, liquidity, and stability over potential returns. Here are some options suitable for investing your emergency fund:

High-Yield Savings Account: A high-yield savings account offered by banks or online financial institutions is one of the safest options for your emergency fund. These accounts typically offer competitive interest rates while providing easy access to your funds when needed.

Money Market Account: Money market accounts are similar to savings accounts but often offer slightly higher interest rates. They provide liquidity and stability to your deposits.

Certificates of Deposit (CDs): CDs offer higher interest rates than savings accounts or money market accounts but require you to lock in your funds for a specific period, ranging from a few months to several years. Look for CDs with relatively short terms to maintain liquidity in case of emergencies.

Short-Term Treasury Securities: Treasury bills (T-bills) are short-term debt securities issued by the central government. They are considered extremely safe investments and can be purchased directly from the Treasury or through a brokerage account. T-bills typically have maturities ranging from a few days to one year.

Short-Term Municipal Bonds: Municipal bonds issued by state or local governments can offer tax advantages for certain investors. Look for short-term municipal bond funds or individual bonds with high credit quality to minimize risk.

Liquid Money Market Mutual Funds: Money market mutual funds invest in short-term, low-risk securities such as government bonds and high-quality corporate debt. They offer liquidity and stability similar to money market accounts but may have slightly higher yields.

Online Savings Accounts with ATM Access: Some online banks offer savings accounts with ATM access, allowing you to withdraw cash quickly in case of emergencies while still earning a competitive interest rate.

When choosing where to invest your emergency fund, prioritize safety, liquidity, and accessibility. Avoid investments with high volatility or lock-up periods that could prevent you from accessing your funds when needed.

How much should be the Emergency Fund:

Individual circumstances, such as income level, monthly expenses, financial commitments, and risk tolerance, all influence the appropriate size of an emergency fund. A typical recommendation is to aim for three to six months' worth of living expenses, nevertheless. The following formula can be used to determine an exact amount for your emergency fund :

Calculate Monthly Expenses: Add up all your essential monthly expenses, including housing costs, utilities, groceries, transportation, insurance premiums, debt payments, and other necessary expenditures. Exclude discretionary expenses that you could cut back on during an emergency.

Assess Your Income Stability: Consider the stability of your income sources. If you have a steady job with little risk of unemployment or income disruption, you may lean towards a smaller emergency fund. On the other hand, if your income is variable or you work in an industry prone to layoffs, a larger emergency fund may be necessary.

Factor in Financial Obligations: Take into account any additional financial obligations you may have, such as medical expenses, insurance deductibles, or potential home or car repairs. These expenses should be covered by your emergency fund as well.

Consider Personal Factors: Reflect on your individual circumstances, such as the number of dependents you have, any special needs or medical conditions, and your comfort level with risk. These factors can influence the size of your emergency fund.

Adjust for Unforeseen Events: While 3 to 6 months' worth of expenses is a general guideline, some experts recommend saving even more for individuals with higher risk factors or those who want additional peace of mind. Factors such as geographic location, industry volatility, and access to credit can also influence your emergency fund target.

Review Periodically: Periodically reassess your emergency fund needs as your financial situation changes. Major life events such as marriage, childbirth, job changes, or significant changes in expenses should prompt a review of your emergency fund size.

By following these guidelines and adjusting the amount of your emergency fund to your own situation, you can make sure you have enough cash on hand to confidently weather unforeseen costs or interruptions in income.

Understanding Investment

The act of purchasing an asset is referred to as investing. The market offers a wide variety of investment options. Investing is the process of buying something with the intention of making money off of it. An asset can be used to generate income through appreciation or regular income. The rise in an asset's value over time is called appreciation. An investor will not use an asset that they have bought for investment purposes. Rather, the investor will use it to make money of it.

The market offers a wide range of investment options. The most well-liked ones are gold, fixed deposits, real estate, stocks and equities. Other well-known investment options include mutual funds, the National Pension Scheme, government and corporate bonds, the Public Provident Fund, exchange-traded funds, and government bonds. Based on the returns they provide, degree of risk, duration, taxation, and whether the returns are guaranteed or market-linked, each of these varies. In the future, we'll examine each of these products in-depth and discuss whether or not to invest in order to achieve the goal of retirement planning.

Prior to selecting an investment option, investors should consider their risk tolerance, goals, investment horizon, and the tax implications of various investment products. They ought to invest in a variety of investment vehicles and never limit themselves to just one. Their portfolio diversification will assist them in distributing their investment risk among various asset classes. Additionally, diversifying your investments within your portfolio will increase portfolio returns. A balanced asset allocation is necessary to achieve the best possible returns. Age, financial objectives, and investor risk tolerance all influence asset allocation.

How is the investment made?

One way to make money work for you is through investing. One hopes to make money from their investments in stocks, bonds, or real estate in the form of dividends, interest, or capital growth. Investing, then, is the act of spending money now on something that will contribute to income generation later on.

Investing is not the same as saving. Savings involves putting money aside for a future need. In contrast, when investing, one buys an asset with the goal of capitalizing on it later on. Refunds from savings won't be high enough to offset inflation. On the other hand, if investing is done correctly, returns can exceed inflation. While investing carries some risk, saving carries none. Savings fits for urgent or short-term objectives. On the other hand, investing works best for long-term and medium-term objectives like retirement planning, marriage, and child education.

Investing entails more than just buying an asset; it also entails doing something that will contribute to future revenue generation. Losing money on an investment is a risk associated with investing. There is always a risk when investing because the goal is to create future income. For instance, if a business is doing well, buying stock in it may seem like a good idea right now. Nonetheless, the company may file for bankruptcy at some point in the future. Therefore, there is always a risk associated with investing. Before deciding to invest in any of the available investment options, investors must be aware of this. Making the right shortlist of investments can be challenging because there are so many options available on the market. Therefore, financial advisors can be hired to assist with investment planning. Even though they charge for their services, financial advisors' knowledge can assist people in reaching their financial objectives.

Investment categories

The market offers a variety of investment options, which we have divided into three primary groups. They are: -

Investments with fixed income: These assets provide interest payments that are guaranteed. These investments carry little risk. A selection of some of the top fixed-income investments is provided below in the next chapter.

Market linked investments: Investments that are linked to the market are those whose returns are reliant on market fluctuations and do not come with a guarantee. These investments carry a high level of risk. But during market rallies, these investments also yield large returns. The top market-linked investment options are explained in the next chapters.

Other investment: Other investments are those that do not fall under the categories of market-linked or fixed income investments. Another name for these is alternative investments. The following chapters will provide an explanation of the list of the most well-liked alternative investment products.

Which is the Suitable Investment for You

We are not cut out to be asset managers or financial experts. Certainly, we don't want to add any more difficulties to the list of difficulties that come with everyday living! But fundamental understanding of investing and investment possibilities should be our goal. With this knowledge, we will be able to distinguish between options that are and are not relevant when evaluating investments. It can enable us to look beyond the data that has been given to us in search of solutions that will lead to the best possible investment choices. We will be forced to examine, scrutinize, and evaluate specifics in order to make well-informed investing decisions as opposed to being influenced by eye-catching figures and optimistic forecasts. Working with professionals and service providers will enable us to select the finest investment solutions for our needs. Therefore, the most important step to guaranteeing a safe and secure financial future is to become an informed investor.

We have previously covered a number of the areas of investment planning that are necessary for our retirement corpus in the earlier chapters. The eighth marvel of the world is the power of compounding, which we have understood. I'm very sure we've covered and comprehended what "investments" are all about to some extent. We will go into great detail about the commonly talked and favored investment possibilities in the market in the upcoming chapters. These investment options, each with a unique mix of advantages and disadvantages, cater to various financial needs and preferences.

In order to accumulate the necessary retirement corpus, you must review all of your investment options and select ones based on your required corpus, risk tolerance, and available time frame. Consider this information as a starting point for your journey towards accumulating a corpus for your fantastic second inning, which is retirement. Use it to assess your present and prospective investments. You should be able to determine the best investment possibilities if you have determined your needed corpus quantity, your risk tolerance, and the amount of time you have to accumulate the necessary corpus. In the upcoming chapters of this book, let's take a closer look at the numerous investing possibilities available.

Bank Fixed Deposits (FDs)

Banks and other financial institutions typically offer fixed deposits, or FDs as they are more commonly known. A fixed deposit is a deposit made in full to your bank for a predetermined period of time at a predetermined interest rate. You get your initial investment back at the end of the term, plus compound interest. Another name for FDs is term deposits. Fixed deposits (FDs) are regarded as one of the safest methods to invest hard-earned money in India. Not only are FDs simple to start, but they also yield healthy returns. Investing in an FD is one of the greatest choices if one's top priority is to save money in order to achieve their financial goals without taking on any risks and with guaranteed returns. In simple words , Fixed Deposits are No Risk or we can say Low Risk Investment options.

Fixed Deposit (FD): What is it?

A fixed deposit is a kind of deposit where a certain amount of money is held for a predetermined amount of time. On the other hand, the investor chooses how long the fixed deposit will last. This term could be several years or just a few days. Fixed deposits offer a set rate of interest to the depositor in exchange for locking in these funds. The account holder or depositor receives the invested principal amount plus maturity interest when the term comes to an end.

One of the most well-liked investment options in India is a fixed deposit, especially among middle-class investors who are risk averse. What is the process for a fixed deposit? Let's examine this.

How Are Fixed Deposit Accounts Operational?

To do that, we must acknowledge that two parties are at play in this situation. The bank is one, and the client is the other. Banks require capital, which they lend to borrowers at interest. Banks primarily receive that money from their clients through a variety of accounts, including savings and current accounts.

Fixed deposits, which come with predetermined interest rates, are one way to get that cash. They lend the money to borrowers at a marginally higher interest rate. The spread, or the bank's earnings, is the difference between the interest rate on FDs and loans.

What is the process for a fixed deposit?

There are numerous options available to you if you want to invest in fixed deposits with some extra cash. The length of time you can deposit money varies from a few days to several years. Naturally, shorter-term interest rates will be less than longer-term fixed deposit interest rates. For instance, the interest rate on a 30-day fixed-rate loan (FD) might be about 6%. The interest rate may be 7% if the deposit is made for a full year.

It may be necessary to compare interest rates offered by various banks in order to get the best deal. Still, the disparities are usually negligible. Interest rates offered by smaller banks, such as cooperative banks, might be higher than those of larger banks. But you have to keep in mind that returns and risk are directly related. There is always a higher risk associated with high interest rates.

Your decision to invest in a fixed deposit or not will rely on your tolerance for risk and the kind of returns you are willing to accept. Fixed deposit returns are typically lower than those of other investment avenues, such as equity, but they also carry fewer risks.

Fixed Deposit (FD) Benefits

The advantages of fixed deposits are as follows:

Guaranteed Rate of Return

Interest Tax Threshold

Adaptable Tenure

Simple Liquidation

Fixed Deposit (FD) Types

There are various kinds of fixed deposit schemes available in India. Depending on one's financial objectives, one can invest in any one or more of these FD types.

A few of the FDs for which an application may be made are listed below:

Cumulative Fixed Deposit: In accordance with guidelines set forth by the Reserve Bank of India, interest on term deposits is to be computed at quarterly compounding intervals and paid at a rate determined by the bank based on the length of the deposit. The depositor in this scheme has the advantage of earning interest on both the principal and interest components (compounding of interest).

Non-cumulative Fixed Deposit: This plan or product pays the depositor interest on a regular basis instead of accumulating it. This guarantees the depositor a passive income. This kind of fixed deposit pays interest on a regular basis; the frequency of payments varies based on the terms of the FD and can be monthly, quarterly, semi-annually, or annually.

Tax Saving Fixed Deposit: Under Section 80C of the Income Tax Act of 1961, these fixed deposits are deductible and have a five-year lock-in period. According to income tax guidelines, the maximum deduction that can be claimed is up to Rs. 1,50,000 /- per year.

Flexi Fixed Deposit: Certain savings and current account schemes offer the Auto Sweep feature, which allows balances above a predetermined threshold to be swept out to Flexi Deposits in multiple sweep out accounts (the threshold, sweep out amount, and deposit period vary depending on the scheme).The FFD may be broken in accordance with the bank's guidelines using the last in, first out (LIFO) principle (in multiples of the sweep amount particular to the scheme) whenever the balance in the savings or current account falls short of the stipulated balance requirement to settle any debits in the operative account.

How Can a Fixed Deposit (FD) Account Be Opened?

Fixed deposit accounts can be opened in one of three ways:

1) by going to the closest bank branch,

2) via net banking, or

3) by using the bank's mobile application.

For whom is FD eligible?

The following qualifications apply to open a fixed deposit account:

A person acting on his own behalf.

Multiple people under one joint name.

minors ten years of age and older on the conditions the bank specifies. Accounts may also be opened in a minor's name with their parent(s) acting as a guardian.

Clubs, associations, partnerships, educational institutions, and joint stock companies—as long as they are legally recognized and the bank is convinced that the account was opened with the intention of saving money.

Documents Needed to Make a Fixed Deposit

The following paperwork is needed to open a fixed deposit account:

The officially valid document, or OVD, that the customer needs to finish the KYC process with is something like this:

The travel document (passport)

The driver's license

Evidence of having an Aadhaar number

The voter identity card that the Indian Election Commission issues

Job card from NREGA duly signed by a state government official Letter from the National Population Register with name and address information

Additionally, the account's constitution determines which documents are needed to complete the KYC.

How is Fixed Deposit (FD) Interest Calculated ?

There are two methods for calculating the interest on a fixed deposit (FD): compound interest (CI) and simple interest (SI).

Depending on the amount deposited and the tenure, banks may compute interest on FDs using either of the two methods.

The following formula is used to calculate interest under the SI method:

S.I. is equal to $(P\times R\times T)/100$.

where P stands for principal, T for time period (in years), and I for interest rate.

Let's say Mr. Sharma invests Rs. 5,000 for four years at a rate of 7% annually. Sharma will be able to apply for the S.I. formula in order to determine the interest he will receive over the course of four years:

Step 1: 5,000 x 7 x 4 = Rs. 140,000
Step 2: Earn Rs. 1,400 in interest by dividing 140,000 by 100.

The following formula is used to calculate interest under the CI method:

P {(1+i/100)n -1} is the CI.

where n is the number of years, P is the principal amount, and i is the interest rate.

Say Mr. Ahuja invests Rs. 7,000 for five years at an annual percentage rate of 8%. Next, using the CI formula, one can determine how much interest Mr. Ahuja will receive under the CI method:

3,285 (7,000{(1+8/100)5 -1}) = Rs.3285.29

Consequently, Rs 3285.29 will be the interest earned.

Taxation on Fixed Deposit income:

The Income Tax Act of 1961 makes the returns on FDs taxable. The interest that is accumulated on the FD is taxed in accordance with the investor's income tax slab provisions and falls under the "income from other sources" category.

In addition, banks deduct 10% TDS when the interest is credited to the investor's FD account if the total interest earned on the FD exceeds Rs. 40,000 for individuals (apart from senior citizens).

The threshold amount for senior citizens is Rs. 50,000. TDS will not be subtracted from the interest amount if the total interest earned on the FD is less than Rs. 40,000. But the interest would be subject to taxation based on the investor's income tax bracket.

A person is required to provide their PAN details to the relevant bank if their interest income from an FD exceeds Rs. 40,000.

In these situations, failure to provide one's PAN card will result in a 20% TDS on FD interest being subtracted from the total interest amount. Following this, income will be taxed based on the income tax slab.

The afore mentioned points could change based on current policies.

Frequently Asked Questions (FAQs)

1. Can FDs be transferred?

FDs can be transferred between the same bank's branches. You need to get in touch with the branch manager of the bank where your FD was made and submit an application for a transfer in writing, along with the receipt for your FD. The account will be moved to the branch of your choice after verification.

It is not possible to move FDs between banks. You will have to open a new FD at a different bank and prematurely close the existing one from the bank in such a scenario.

2. What happens if the account holder passes away before the account matures?

The nominee may claim the maturity amount in the event that the account holder is not living at the time of maturity. In the event that the investor failed to designate a nominee, the surviving family member must present a succession certificate or proof of legal heirship in order to receive the maturity amount.

3. How much can be deposited, both minimum and maximum, for FDs?

Banks have different minimum deposits required for fixed-rate accounts. Furthermore, there is no cap on the total amount of money that can be invested in FD.

4. What is a nomination for an FD?

The process of designating a nominee for an FD involves the account holder choosing someone who will be able to withdraw the maturity amount in the event of the account holder's death.

Deposit Insurance:

Each bank depositor is covered for the principal and interest amounts they hold in the same right and same up to a maximum of 5,00,000 (Rupees Five Lakhs). Deposit insurance up to Rs 5 lakh is offered by the Reserve

Bank of India (RBI) subsidiary Deposit Insurance and Credit Guarantee Corporation (DICGC). Account types covered by this coverage include current accounts, savings accounts, fixed deposits, and recurring deposits. The following banks are insured: All Nationalized Banks, State Cooperative Banks, District Central Cooperative Banks, Urban Cooperative Banks, Private Sector Banks, Foreign Banks in India, Local Area Banks, Small Finance Banks, Payment Banks, Regional Rural Banks, and cooperative banks.The DICGC does not provide insurance for primary cooperative societies.

Printed pamphlets detailing the protections provided by the Corporation to the insured banks' depositors are provided to the banks by the DICGC upon their registration as insured banks. If in doubt, the depositor should specifically ask the branch official this question.

Why should you invest in Fixed Deposits: -

One of the most reliable and secure investment options offered by banks is a fixed deposit. It offers guaranteed returns, a competitive interest rate, and additional advantages like safety and liquidity to investors. One of the most reliable and secure investment options offered by banks is a fixed deposit. Even though there are a lot of alternative investment options, most investors still consider this traditional instrument to be among the best. The following are some justifications for investing in FDs:-

i) Promised Returns

Market dynamics have no effect on FD accounts, in contrast to other investment types. This is the main explanation for why they are regarded as a secure investment choice. Depending on the interest rate the bank offers, investors can be confident that their hard-earned money will generate healthy returns. Setting financial goals also helps a lot because it lets you know how much money you will grow in a given amount of time.

ii) A favorable interest rate

Good interest rates are a major factor in the popularity of fixed deposits. The interest rate on FDs is typically higher than that of savings accounts. Seniors who invest in FDs also pay a higher interest rate than other investors.

iii) **FD Is Simple to Invest in**

Investing in a fixed deposit is hassle-free. All you have to do is complete an application and send it in with the payment. You can visit your closest branch or open an FD account online from the comfort of your home. By choosing the multi-deposit facility, you can even invest in multiple FDs at once.

iv) **Simple to Keep Track of**

You don't need to routinely check on the performance of the FD interest rate because it stays constant for the duration of the loan. On the other hand, you must monitor its maturity date. Additionally, a few banks provide auto-renewal. When the FD matures under this arrangement, the bank will automatically renew it.

Note: You can change the command before the deposit matures if you have chosen to have it automatically renew.

v) **Permits Early Withdrawal**

FDs may be withdrawn whenever necessary. You will always have a certain amount of money, even though there will be a penalty.

vi) **provides a sweep-in and nomination feature.**

Fixed deposits provide the option to nominate. When opening the FD account, you have the option to submit the nomination right away. You do, however, have the freedom to modify the nomination whenever it is more convenient for you as the account holder. You make use of the sweep-in feature as well. You won't have to worry about a cheque bouncing or not having enough money in your account to complete a transaction when you have a sweep-in facility. For many years, fixed deposits have been the preferred investment option for the majority of Indians. Extremely adaptable and flexible, this financial product aids in instilling a commitment to saving.

Post Office Fixed Deposit

No Risk / Low Risk Investment option :

The largest postal department in the world, the Department of Post is regarded as the foundation of India's communications network. The department is expanding its operations and reach by branching out into a number of industries, including retail services, money transfers, insurance, and more. The largest and oldest banking institution in the nation is the Post Office Savings Scheme. The Department of Posts handles the Post Office Savings programs on behalf of the Ministry of Finance.

Post Office FD is one of the most sought-after schemes in the nation since it has a low risk element and guarantees returns on deposits. The program has a number of advantages, such as the flexibility to move an account from one post office to another and the choice to extend the deposit upon maturity. Additionally, maturity profits that are not withdrawn are qualified for a two-year savings account interest rate. With the option to earn annual interest at compound interest rates, fixed deposit tenures range from one, two, and three years to five years. For the post office FD plan, an automatic credit facility with interest is offered to the savings bank account.

For post office fixed deposits, early closure and withdrawal are permitted following the completion of six months from the deposit's start date. There will be a penalty if the deposit account is closed before it matures, though.

A Post Office Fixed Deposit account can be opened with a minimum of Rs. 200 and an unlimited maximum amount. A friend, family member, or relative might be nominated while opening a fixed deposit account. You can choose to renew or withdraw the balance when your account matures. The sum can also be withdrawn prior to the maturity of your account, although doing so will incur fees. In the event that you did not choose the new tax regime plan, you will benefit tax-wise. The Income Tax Act of 1961's Section 80C will apply to the tax deductions. Under Section 80TTB, senior citizens are eligible for a tax exemption of up to Rs. 50,000.

For investors who have a large sum to deposit for a set amount of time, post office time deposits are designed. Because the scheme has government backing, it is not just low risk but also provides excellent capital protection. As a result, the investment increases with guaranteed returns at a predetermined rate. There are no big returns if the provided interest rate is higher than inflation. As such, the plan is not immune to inflation. Every year, before April 1st, the interest rate for a five-year deposit are generally announced. With a 0.25% margin, it is often in line with G-sec rates of comparable maturities. Since the scheme is offered by the government of India, it does not require any commercial rating. A person may take out a loan against the deposit or take it out early.

Company Fixed Deposit

Risk Category – High Risk

Corporate Fixed Deposits (corporate FDs) are term deposits held for a predetermined amount of time at predetermined interest rates. Financial and non-banking financial companies (NBFCs) offer company fixed deposits. Different company fixed deposits have maturities ranging from a few months to a few years. Corporate FDs are riskier than bank FDs because they are unsecured and usually not secured by collateral. Company FDs are governed by company law; however, banks and NBFCs are subject to strict regulation by the Reserve Bank of India (RBI), which periodically assesses their performance.

High safety against the principal and interest payment default risk is indicated by credit ratings. A company may receive ratings such as AAA, AA, BBB, etc. based on a variety of factors. Your money is protected when you invest in company FDs thanks to these regulations.

Corporate Fixed Deposits are only subject to taxation if interest income surpasses Rs. 5,000. The TDS rate is 10% if the interest received exceeds Rs.5,000 (provided PAN details are given). 20% TDS deduction on FD interest is due if PAN information is not submitted.

A bank fixed deposit has a term that can last anywhere from months to years, which is a lot longer than a company fixed deposit. Bank fixed deposits are better than corporate fixed deposits if you want to invest in fixed deposits for a longer duration—up to ten years. Generally speaking, corporate FDs have a shorter penalty period than bank FDs. For instance, if you choose to take your money out of a bank before the maturity period, you would be penalized. In the meanwhile, there is only a three-month penalty for early withdrawal of FDs from certain corporate.

The security of the deposit is another distinction. The DICGC insures bank deposits up to Rs. 5 lakh per depositor per bank. This implies that you can receive your money back from DICGC up to Rs. 5 lakh in the event of a bank failure. Corporate FDs, on the other hand, are more vulnerable to issuer default because they are not insured by any agency. Consequently, before making an investment in a corporate FD, it is crucial to verify the credit rating.

The way interest income is treated tax-wise is another distinction. If the interest income from a corporate or bank deposit account (FD) surpasses Rs. 40,000 (or Rs. 50,000 for senior citizens) in a financial year, 10% tax deducted at source (TDS) will be applied. However, if your total income is less than the taxable limit, bank FDs also have the option to submit Form 15G or 15H to avoid TDS. Since corporate FDs lack this choice, TDS is withheld regardless of your income level.

PROS for investing in Corporate FD:

The primary benefit of purchasing corporate FDs is their propensity to yield larger returns than bank FDs. Corporate FDs provide you with set, predictable returns that assist you guarantee your financial security during periods of significant market volatility and uncertain returns. The greater tenure and amount flexibility that corporate FDs give is another benefit of investing in them. You can select a tenure based on your liquidity requirements and financial objectives. Additionally, you can select an amount between Rs. 5,000 and Rs. 1 crore or more, depending on what your savings budget allows. The fact that corporate FDs provide a range of payment possibilities for your interest income is another benefit of investing in them. You have two options: the non-cumulative option, where the interest is paid monthly, quarterly, half-yearly, or annually depending on your preference, or the cumulative option, where the interest is compounded quarterly or annually and paid at maturity together with the principle.

CONS for investing in Corporate FD:

Investing in corporate FDs has a larger risk than bank FDs, which is its principal drawback. Corporate fixed deposits (FDs) are comparatively riskier than bank FDs since, as was previously indicated, they are not covered by the DICGC.

In conclusion, corporate FDs have a larger credit risk even though they have the potential to yield larger profits than bank FDs. Before making an investment, carefully weigh the benefits and drawbacks, learn as much as you can about the creditworthiness of the issuing company, and speak with a financial counselor to be sure your goals and risk tolerance are compatible.

Public Provident Fund (PPF)

Risk Category – No Risk

PPF offers total capital protection and assured, risk-free profits because it is supported by the Indian government. There is very little or No danger associated with owning a PPF account. PPF accounts are utilized as a technique for portfolio diversification by investors since their set returns make them attractive.

The National Savings Institute of the Ministry of Finance launched the Public Provident Fund (PPF), an instrument in India that allows savings while reducing taxes. It was established in 1968. The scheme's primary goal is to encourage small savings by providing an investment with respectable returns along with advantages related to income tax. The Central Government is the one offering the program. **The Government Savings Banks Act of 1873 prohibits any court order or decree from attaching any balance in a PPF account.** To recover unpaid taxes, Income Tax and other government agencies may attach the account.

Eligibility: -

Residents of India are able to open Public Provident Fund accounts and receive tax-free returns on their contributions.

Returns on investment:

There is a 500 rupee minimum annual deposit required to start and maintain a PPF account. A PPF account holder (including accounts for which the account holder acts as guardian) may deposit money into their account up to Rs. 1.5 lacs per financial year. A guardian must be present when underage children's PPF accounts are opened in their names. Parents can act as minor children's guardians in these PPF accounts. Interest on deposits over Rs. 1.5 lacs won't be paid within a fiscal year. The money can be deposited entirely at once or in equal amounts each year. However, this does not mean that a single deposit is made once a month.

The PPF account interest rate is released by the Indian government's Ministry of Finance on a quarterly basis. This interest is compounded annually and paid in March of each year. Interest is calculated each month using the balance that is lowest at the conclusion of the fifth and last day of the month.

The Scheme's duration:

There is a fifteen-year initial run-time. Subsequently, the subscriber is left with two choices: either it closes and the entire sum is taken out, or it can be prolonged for one or more five-year blocks, either with or without further payments.

Options for PPF maturity: -

After the maturity period has passed, the subscriber has three options.

Total Withdrawal: subscriber have an option for complete withdrawal on maturity.

Extend the PPF account without making any contributions: PPF accounts are renewable after 15 years, and subscribers are not required to make any additional contributions after the account matures. This is the default option, meaning it will activate automatically if the subscriber does nothing within a year of the maturity of his PPF account. If the option to extend without making a contribution is selected, any amount can be taken out of the PPF account. The only limitation is that each financial year, only one withdrawal is allowed. The remaining sum continues to accrue interest.

Extend the PPF account and make a contribution: This option allows the subscriber to fund the account after it has been extended. In order to select this option, the subscriber must submit Form H to the bank where they currently have a PPF account within a year of the maturity date (i.e., before the 16-year PPF term is up). With this option, the subscriber's maximum withdrawal during the five-year period is 60% of the PPF amount (the amount in the PPF account at the start of the extended period). Only one withdrawal is allowed per year.

Loans: -

The loan facility is offered from the third to the fifth fiscal year. The interest rate applied to a loan taken out by a PPF account subscriber on or after December 12, 2019, will be one percent higher than the current PPF interest rate.

The 2019 Public Provident Fund Scheme has lowered the interest spread from the previous 2 percent to 1 (one) percent.

A loan of up to twenty-five percent of the remaining amount at the end of the second year immediately prior would be permitted. Repayment for these withdrawals must be made within 36 months.

If you are within the third year and before the sixth, you may apply for a second loan, but only after the first has been completely paid back. It should be noted that no loans would be allowed after you were eligible for withdrawals. Loans are not available for accounts that have been closed or are no longer active.

Features: -

The central government creates the public provident fund. Any nationalized bank, certain approved private bank, or post office is willing to allow account openings. Any individual, even a minor, may open an account in their name.

i) The smallest sum that can be deposited is Rs. 500.
ii) As of April 2023, the interest rate stands at 7.1% annually.
iii) Taxes are not applied to interest earned.
iv) Upon maturity, the entire balance may be withdrawn.
v) Currently, the maximum amount that can be deposited into an account annually is Rs.150,000.
vi) Annual compound interest is earned on the PPF subscription.
vii) The entire amount that builds up over time is free from wealth tax.

Withdrawals from PPF Account: -

The money can be fully withdrawn following the maturity period, after a 15-year lock-in period. On the other hand, early withdrawals are permitted beginning with the seventh fiscal year. 50% of the balance in the account at the end of the fourth year prior to the current year, or the end of the year immediately prior, whichever is less, is the maximum amount that can be withdrawn prematurely.

The entire PPF amount, including the interest amount, can be withdrawn tax-free after 15 years of maturity.

Nomination: -

The ability to nominate someone in the name of one or more people is available. The subscriber may also define the nominees' shares.

PPF Penalty / Revival / Nomination:

The account will be closed if the required minimum contribution is not made in any given year. Each year that the bearer is inactive, they must pay a penalty of Rs.50 to be activated. Additionally, he or she must deposit Rs. 500 for each year that the account is inactive.

The remaining amount will be paid to the account holder's nominee or legal heir even if it happens before the 15-year mark. The deceased's account cannot be continued by nominees or legal heirs.

If a deceased person's account balance exceeds Rs.150,000, the nominee or legal heir must provide identification in order to be eligible to receive the money.

Premature PPF account closure: -

In order to make the early closure of PPF accounts easier, the Public Provident Fund (Amendment) Scheme, 2016 modified Paragraph 9 for Sub-Rule 3(C) of the Public Provident Fund Scheme, 1968. After five years, an early closure of a PPF account is allowed for the account holder's higher education or for the medical treatment of family members. Nevertheless, there is a 1% interest rate penalty for early closure. According to GOI NOTICES dated December 12, 2019, there are some new regulations regarding early withdrawal.

- If there is a change in residency, the account may be closed unless a valid passport and visa are presented.
- Higher education for oneself or a dependent that requires payment Letter accounts may close if bills or admissions verify them. The remaining rules apply in the event of the holder's passing or a dependent's illness.

Transfer of PPF Account: -

Upon request, the subscriber may transfer their account to another branch, bank, or post office, or vice versa. There is no cost for the service.

Step 1: Go to the bank or post office location where the PPF account is kept and request the transfer form. You will be given a form to fill out by the bank or post office.

Step 2: The certified copy of the account, the nomination form, the specimen signature, and the account opening application will then be forwarded by the current bank. Additionally, it will forward the cheque or direct deposit for the balance owed on the PPF account to the new bank at the customer's designated branch.

Step 3: Your bank will notify you and request that you submit a new PPF account opening form and the old PPF passbook as soon as it receives these documents. Nominations for this new account are also welcome. The KYC documents must also be submitted by you.

Step 4: Check if the transferred PPF account appears under the PPF account tab or link in your login after a few weeks if you have internet banking access with your bank. Inquire at the nearby bank branch if that isn't the case.

Tax Concessions: -

Under the previous tax system, annual contributions were eligible for a tax deduction under Section 80C of income tax. The annual tax benefit is limited to Rs. 1.50 lacs.

PPF is included in the tax basket under EEE (Exempt, Exempt, Exempt). Under Section 80C of the Income Tax Act, contributions made to PPF accounts were eligible for tax benefits under the previous tax regime. Income tax is not applied to interest earned, and there is no tax applied to maturity proceeds.

National Pension System (NPS)

Risk Category – Medium / High Risk

NPS investments are vulnerable to market volatility. The Schemes' and Pension Funds' historical performance is in no way a guarantee of their future results. No returns are guaranteed or assured by NPS Trust. Future returns may be impacted by changes in tax benefits and government regulations.

The NPS is the most underutilized of all the investment options open to Indian savers. The NPS has the greatest disparity among all investment classes between how well-suited it is for every saver and how little it is used.

Every saver's main long-term investment should be in the NPS. It should be prioritized above all other investments once you have finished with your emergency fund, term insurance, and health coverage. In this section, let's examine NPS in more detail. I think the NPS will draw more investors as a result of its favorable returns, comparative security, and accessibility. A growing number of people will decide to direct their flexible savings towards the NPS over time. The change points to growing confidence and enthusiasm in the NPS as a dependable and advantageous platform for savings. I hope our readers treat the NPS with the same respect they do all other types of investments.

The National Pension System (NPS) is a voluntary, defined contribution retirement savings scheme that enables subscribers to make the best decisions for their future by making systematic savings throughout their working lives. The NPS aims to instill in citizens the habit of saving for retirement. The National Pension System (NPS) is administered and regulated by the Pension Fund Regulatory and Development Authority (PFRDA), which was established by the PFRDA Act of 2013. NPS is a defined contribution product with a market link. The Central Recordkeeping Agency (CRA) generates and maintains a unique Permanent Retirement Account Number (PRAN) for each individual subscriber under NPS.

Why is the National Pension System the best retirement option?

According to tax and investment experts, NPS offered a more affordable investment model than other annuity plans on the market, as well as income tax benefits. Aside from that, NPS is a government-backed scheme that also provides social security after retirement. Aside from the tax benefits, NPS is a good investment option if you want to grow your wealth and build a solid retirement corpus.

The System:

NPS has two types of accounts: Tier-I and Tier-II. Tier-I accounts are pension accounts with limited withdrawals. Tier-II is a voluntary account that allows for investment and withdrawal liquidity. It is only permitted if the subscriber has an active Tier-I account in his or her name. Contributions accumulate over time and grow with market-linked returns until retirement.

On exit/retirement/superannuation, a minimum of 40% of the corpus is required to be used to obtain a lifetime pension by purchasing an annuity from a life insurance company, with the remaining corpus paid as a lump sum.

NPS Platform:

The NPS platform provides various models to cater to various user segments. These are some examples:
The Government Model for Central and State Government Employees • NPS is mandatory for Central Government employees (except the Armed Forces) hired on or after January 1, 2004. As a result, with the exception of West Bengal, all state governments have adopted NPS for their employees. Employees of the government make a monthly contribution of 10% of their salary, and the government matches it. With effect from April 1, 2019, the employer contribution rate for central government employees has been increased to 14%.

The Corporate Model:

Companies can adopt NPS for their employees with contribution rates as per the employment conditions.

The All Citizens Model:

The All Citizens Model of the NPS allows all citizens of India aged between 18 - 60 years to join NPS on voluntary basis.

NPS Architecture:

NPS is administered through an unbundled architecture involving intermediaries appointed by the PFRDA viz. Pension Funds, Custodian, Central Recordkeeping Agency (CRA), National Pension System Trust, Trustee Bank, Points of Presence (PoP) and Annuity Service Providers (ASPs).

Who is eligible for NPS scheme?

The employees of the corporate entity, enrolled by the employer having Indian Citizenship between the age of 18-60 years and complying with the KYC norms, are eligible to be registered as subscribers under NPS.

Subscribers to the NPS private model can come from both the organized and unorganized sectors (including self-employed, traders, and business owners). Under this model, an NRI can also subscribe to the NPS.

How do I open an NPS account?

Online mode:

To register online, go to the eNPS website (https://enps.nsdl.com/eNPS/NationalPensionSystem.html). The NPS account must be linked to your mobile number, Aadhaar, and Permanent Account Number (PAN). An OTP will be sent to your registered mobile number to complete the validation.The following documents are required for an NPS account: ZIP file containing Aadhaar Paperless Offline e-KYC. PAN and cancelled cheque scanned in jpeg, jpg, png, and pdf formats.

Offline NPS Account Registration.

To open an NPS Account Offline, go to the nearest PFRDA-registered Point of Presence (POP) to get the registration form. POPs are banks and financial institutions that have been appointed by the PFRDA to provide services to customers under the NPS scheme. To open an NPS account, you must bring your KYC documents and bank information with you.

Important Features of NPS: -

Access and portability are ensured by online access to the pension account for NPS subscribers via web portal and mobile app, across all geographical locations, and portability of employments.

Partial withdrawal- Subscribers may withdraw up to 25% of their own contributions at any time before exiting NPS Tier-I for a maximum of three times during the entire tenure of subscription under NPS for specified purposes. After contributing for at least ten years, partial withdrawals from NPS Tier-1 are permitted, with a minimum five-year gap between successive withdrawals.

Tax advantages available through NPS:

a) Employee contributions to NPS Tier I are tax deductible under section 80 CCD (1) of the Income Tax Act, up to a maximum of Rs. 1.50 lakh under section 80 C of the Income Tax Act. From fiscal year 2015-16, the subscriber is entitled to a tax deduction in addition to the deduction allowed under section 80CCD(1) for contributions to an NPS Tier I account, up to a maximum of Rs. 50,000 under section 80CCD 1(B).

b) Employer contributions to NPS Tier-I are tax deductible under Income Tax Act Section 80CCD (2) (14% of salary for central government employees and 10% for others). This rebate is in addition to the limit set forth in Section 80C.

c) An interim/partial withdrawal of up to 25% of the subscriber's NPS Tier-I contributions is tax-free.

d) As of 1.4.2019, lump sum withdrawals from NPS Tier-I of up to 60% of total pension wealth are tax exempt at the time of superannuation.

e) A minimum of 40% of the amount spent on an annuity purchased from an Annuity Service Provider registered and regulated by the Insurance Regulatory and Development Authority (IRDA) and empanelled by PFRDA is also tax exempt.

Nomination facility:

You can name a nominee when you open an NPS account. You should have a nominee for all of your investments, including your NPS account. An NPS account can have up to three nominees, according to the PFRDA.

NPS subscribers should keep in mind that they should only nominate specific individuals to their NPS account.

If the deceased subscriber's nomination is not registered prior to his death, all of their pension wealth accumulated over the time period will be paid to their family.

Gold / Sovereign Gold Bonds / Gold ETF

Risk Category: Gold (Low) , SGB (Low) , Gold ETF (Medium – Market Risk)

Why should you invest in gold?

Gold is a wealth symbol. It has traditionally been regarded as a hedge against inflation, moving in tandem with rising inflation and, more specifically, the dollar. Because of its low to negative correlation with all other major asset classes, gold is a highly effective portfolio diversifier. Gold has had no statistically significant correlation with equities over the last 25 years. The fundamental reason for this low correlation is that the factors influencing gold prices are not the same as those influencing other asset returns. While gold has no statistically significant correlation with mainstream asset classes, there is evidence that when equities are under stress, or when share markets fall, an inverse correlation can develop between gold and equities.

In contrast to currencies that have seen significant fluctuation, the value of goods and services that gold can buy has remained largely stable. A detailed study of around 350 years revealed that the basket of goods that gold could buy remained constant. Gold protects your portfolio from volatility because the factors that influence the returns of most asset classes have little impact on the price of gold. The risk of volatility in a portfolio can be reduced by adding gold to it for a given level of returns. Similarly, turbulent situations such as global economic turmoil or even the occurrence of war always have a negative impact on the prices of most asset classes, with the exception of gold, which has a positive impact on gold prices. This is due to increased demand for gold as a safe haven for funds. It is the only medium of exchange that is completely free of credit risk because it does not imply liability on the part of the other entity.

The primary reasons for including gold in your portfolio are:

- Gold improves the stability and predictability of portfolio returns. It is not correlated with other assets because the price of gold is not always driven by the same factors that drive the performance of other assets.
- Adding gold to a portfolio introduces a completely new asset class. Gold is unusual in that it serves as both a commodity and a monetary asset.
- Gold has a history of retaining its value, making it an effective inflation hedge. When the US dollar is underperforming or there is economic and political uncertainty, gold prices tend to rise.
- The most important factor is that gold can provide an important level of diversification to your portfolio, as gold prices have historically shown a negative correlation with other asset classes.

The most important thing to remember is that gold should not be invested to earn a return on investment, but rather as a portfolio diversifier and inflation hedge.

How much should you invest in gold?

You should construct your investment portfolio in such a way that it allows you to meet your long-term financial objectives. As a result, you must develop a financial plan that takes into account your financial objectives, investment horizon, risk tolerance, and current portfolio composition. Ideally, you should allocate 10-15% of your investment portfolio to gold. When deciding how much to invest in gold, keep your overall investment strategy and financial goals in mind. There are times when gold investments appear to be more profitable than stocks, and vice versa. Markets react to macroeconomic events as well as a variety of other factors. As a result, it is critical to monitor and rebalance your portfolio's risk-return balance on a regular basis.

Investing in Gold: -

Traditionally, Indian families would buy gold ornaments, bars, and coins to invest in. With the passage of time, new gold investment options such as Gold ETFs, Paper Gold (Sovereign Gold Bonds), and Multi Asset Funds became popular. While physical gold has advantages and disadvantages, paper gold and gold ETFs do not. We will go over the various gold investment options in depth.

Physical Gold: -

You can invest in gold by buying ornaments, coins, or gold bars. Keep the following tips in mind when purchasing gold ornaments or coins:

Understand The Purity: Carats are used to determine the purity of gold. A 24kt gold piece is 99.9% pure, and the purity decreases as you select 22kt, 18kt, 14kt, and so on. Investing in gold jewelry without first conducting a thorough examination is a no-no. A hallmark is another way to indicate purity, and it is best to buy hallmarked jewelry.

Price: The purity of the jewelry, as well as the alloy it is mixed with and the amount of labor put into the piece, determine the price. It is wise to compare prices before investing, but it is also prudent to purchase from a reputable jeweler or well-known brand.

Colour: The colour gold may have colour variations. Combining pure gold with other metals produces a different colour, but yellow gold is the most popular in our country. If you want more variety, other colors such as white and rose gold are available.

Weight: It is critical to check the weight of the gold you are purchasing before paying for it. Because other used stones can increase the weight, you may end up paying a higher price.

Jewelry with a Hallmark: Investing in gold jewelry is a big decision for most of us because it costs a lot of money. Buying hallmarked jewelry is strongly advised. It not only indicates purity, but it is also a safe investment.

Gold coins are a better investment than jewelry. When compared to ornaments such as earrings and rings, coins allow you to purchase gold in its purest form while incurring lower manufacturing costs. Gold coins serve as a hedge against inflation. You do not have to pay capital gains tax until you sell your gold coins. You can keep your gold investment private if that is important to you. Unlike gold jewelry, gold coins have no manufacturing costs and thus do not lose money value when time is reset. Furthermore, gold purchased from a jeweler will fetch you a lower resale value depending on the market price of gold at the time. You should try to resell your gold coin to the same merchant who sold it to you in the first place. The purest form of gold is 24 Karat (KT), which contains 24 out of 24 parts gold.

Sovereign Gold Bond:

The government launched the Sovereign Gold Bond Scheme (SGB) in November 2015 as part of the Gold Monetization Scheme. The Reserve Bank of India, in consultation with the Government of India, has begun to invest in installments under this scheme. The RBI updates the terms and conditions of this scheme on a regular basis. It used to open for SGB according to the calendar below. The SGB rate announced by the RBI in a press release prior to each new investment.

Features of SGB:

SGBs are issued on behalf of the Government of India by the Reserve Bank of India. The Bonds are denominated in multiples of grams of gold by weight, with 1 gram serving as the unit of measurement. The bonds have an 8-year term and can be withdrawn from the scheme on the interest payment dates in the fifth, sixth, and seventh years. The smallest amount of gold that can be invested is one gram.

In each fiscal year (April-March), the maximum investment limit will be 4 kg for individuals, 4 kg for Hindu Undivided Families, and 20 kg for trusts and similar entities, as notified by the government from time to time. A self-declaration will be made to that effect. The annual limit will include bonds issued by the government as well as those purchased on the secondary market and invested in stages. In the case of a joint holding, the investment limit of 4 kg will only apply to the first applicant.

The bond will be paid in cash (up to Rs.20,000/-) or by Demand Draft, Cheque, or Electronic Banking. Under the Government Securities Act of 2006, the gold bonds will be issued as Government of India stock. For this, investors will be given a holding certificate. The bond is convertible into demat form. The redemption price will be in Indian rupees, based on the simple average of the closing price of gold of 999 purity published by IBJA (Indian Bullion and Jewelers Association) for the previous three business days.

Investors will receive interest at a fixed rate of 2.50 percent per year on the nominal value, payable every six months. Bonds can be used as loan collateral. Loan to Value (LTV) ratio to be brought up to par with

Ordinary Gold Loan as per Reserve Bank instructions issued from time to time. The authorized banks will mark the lien on the Bonds in the depositories. The Bonds will be tradable on stock exchanges within a fortnight of the Reserve Bank of India's notification date.

How can I invest in sovereign gold bonds directly?

Investors who want to invest in sovereign gold bonds must fill out an application form. The form is provided by the issuing banks or can be obtained in person at designated post offices. Investors can also fill out the form by downloading it from the RBI website.

Can I purchase a Sovereign gold bond online?

The issue price of the Gold Bonds is usually Rs. 50 per gram lower for those who subscribe and pay online. The Bonds will be paid for in cash (up to a maximum of Rs. 20,000), demand draft, cheque, or electronic banking.

SGBs are regarded as a superior alternative to physical gold because they allow investors to profit from gold price appreciation while also paying a fixed interest rate of 2.5% per annum payable semi-annually on the nominal value. Furthermore, unlike physical gold, you do not need to be concerned about the safekeeping of SGB.

Gold ETFs (Exchange Traded Funds)

A Gold ETF is an exchange-traded fund (ETF) that seeks to track the price of physical gold . They are gold-based passive investment instruments that invest in gold bullion. In a nutshell, Gold ETFs are units that represent physical gold, which can be paper or dematerialized. One Gold ETF unit is equal to one gram of gold and is backed by very pure physical gold. Gold ETFs combine the flexibility of stock investing with the ease of gold investing.

Gold ETFs, like any other stock, are listed and traded on the National Stock Exchange of India (NSE) and the Bombay Stock Exchange Ltd. (BSE). Gold ETFs, like any other company stock, trade on the cash segment of the BSE and NSE and can be bought and sold at market prices on an ongoing basis.

Purchasing Gold ETFs means purchasing gold in electronic form. Gold ETFs can be bought and sold in the same way that stocks can. When you redeem a Gold ETF, you do not receive physical gold, but rather the cash equivalent. Gold ETFs are traded using a dematerialized account (Demat) and a broker, making it an extremely convenient way to invest in gold electronically.

A Gold ETF's holdings are completely transparent due to its direct gold pricing. Furthermore, because of their unique structure and creation mechanism, ETFs have much lower expenses than physical gold investments.

How Does A Gold ETF Operate?

Pricing: Gold ETF prices are listed on the BSE/NSE websites and can be purchased or sold at any time through a stock broker. Unlike gold jewelry, gold ETFs can be purchased and sold at the same price across India.

Where to buy: Gold ETFs can be purchased on the BSE / NSE through a broker using a demat and trading account. When purchasing or selling gold ETFs, a brokerage fee and minor fund management charges apply.

Risks: Gold ETFs are vulnerable to market risks that affect the price of gold. SEBI Mutual Funds Regulations apply to gold ETFs. A statutory auditor must audit the physical gold purchased by fund houses on a regular basis.

Who Should Purchase A Gold ETF ?

Gold ETFs are ideal for investors who want to invest in gold but do not want to do so in physical gold due to storage issues or concerns about gold purity, and who also want to take advantage of tax breaks. Investors can save money if their investment is significant because there is no premium or making charge. In addition, one unit (one gram) can be purchased for few thousands only.

What Are the Benefits of Buying Gold ETF Units?

- The purity of the gold is guaranteed, and each unit is backed by high-purity physical gold.
- Gold prices are transparent and updated in real time.
- Stock exchange listing and trading.
- Gold is a tax-efficient investment because the income earned from it is treated as long-term capital gain.
- There is no wealth tax, security transaction tax, VAT, or sales tax.

- No need to worry about theft because units are kept safe and secure in a Demat. One also saves money on safe deposit box fees.
- ETFs are accepted as loan collateral.
- There is no entry or exit load. (Read Mutual Fund investment chapter to understand more about entry and exit load).

How Can I Sell Or Redeem A Gold ETF ?

Gold ETFs can be purchased on the stock exchange through a broker with a demat and trading account. ETFs are best used as a tool to benefit from the price of gold rather than to gain access to physical gold because they are backed by physical gold. When one liquidates Gold ETF Units, one is paid according to the domestic market price of gold. AMCs also allow redemption of Gold ETF Units in the form of physical gold in 'Creation Unit' size if the equivalent of 1kg of gold is held in ETFs or multiples thereof.

To have a detailed understand about how ETFs work and operate , Please refer to Mutual Funds (ETF) chapter.

Fixed Income Securities

Each investor has unique requirements. For example, a twenty-three-year-old with an excellent career and no particular financial responsibilities might want to allocate a sizeable portion of his earnings to long-term, high-growth investments.

But not everyone can afford to take significant risks. For example, a pregnant woman may request a guaranteed corpus to finance her child's college education after 15 years. Investment products that can provide fixed returns are necessary in order to meet these requirements. Fixed-income securities can be useful in this situation.

In India, what are fixed income securities?

Debt instruments with a fixed rate of return on investment that are issued by governmental or corporate entities are known as fixed-income securities. Fixed-income securities come in a variety of forms, such as bonds, national savings certificates, mutual funds, and treasury bills.

Certain securities offer recurring returns in order to generate a consistent source of income. Many investors prefer to include these fixed-income instruments in their investment portfolio along with equity and other market-linked instruments because of the fixed returns.

What makes investing in fixed income instruments recommended?

Investors, as previously stated, have varying needs, risk tolerances, and financial objectives. Investors in fixed-income securities, regardless of earning potential, should seek safe returns without following market movements.

People who are setting up a corpus for the wedding of their children or their college education are more likely to take small financial risks in these situations. An appropriate instrument for them will be fixed-income securities.

A person in need of a steady income stream may also want to think about investing in fixed-income securities. For example, those who are getting close to retirement age need to secure a steady stream of income after they leave the workforce. They have access to a variety of fixed-income investment options, which provide fixed payments on a regular basis.

Fixed-income securities are a viable option for portfolio diversification for investors who possess a greater risk tolerance. To put it plainly, you can mitigate the risks involved with equity investments by holding fixed-income securities in your portfolio.

Debt Funds

Risk Category: Fixed-income investments and debt mutual funds have different risk profiles. Debt funds do carry some risk because of credit risk and interest rate risk, even though fixed-income investments are sometimes seen as safer because of their fixed yield and deposit safety.

A type of mutual fund called a debt fund makes money by lending your money to businesses and the government. The length of the loan and the type of borrower establish a debt fund's risk level. Debt funds are an option for investments with a one-day to three-year time horizon. If you invest for at least three years, they provide better post-tax returns than FDs. You should keep your emergency cash in liquid debt funds. With minimal risk, you can outperform savings accounts in terms of returns. These funds combine the assets of investors and use the corpus to purchase bonds, T-bills, and other fixed-income securities.

How do debt funds work: -

Return Sources: There are two ways a debt fund can make money. First, coupon or accrual income is produced by interest payments made on its bond holdings. Second, bond prices move against changes in interest rates, causing capital gains or losses across the fund portfolio. Bond prices drop and the fund's value decreases as market yields rise. Bond prices rise and the fund's value increases when market yields decline. This component of capital gain/loss is also known as the mark-to-market (MTM) return. The kind of bonds that a debt fund holds determines how much it makes in capital gains and interest.

Interest earnings and capital gains: The average maturity of the bonds held by the fund determines the capital gains. Long-term bond prices rise more than those of short-term bonds when market yields decline. Accordingly, funds exhibiting a higher average maturity also exhibit a higher rate of net asset value growth. On the other hand, funds with a longer average maturity experience a more severe decline in valuation when market yields rise. Therefore, the likelihood of capital gains or losses is higher for funds that hold more long-term bonds. To put it in technical terms, longer-duration funds have a higher mark-to-market (MTM) or interest rate risk. Debt funds with a majority stake in short-term bonds exhibit low gains and losses on capital. Their primary source of income is interest payments. These funds hold lower-rated bonds, which can raise yields. This is because, in comparison to bonds with higher ratings, bonds with lower credit ratings—which are more prone to default—have to pay higher coupon rates.

Strategies to Manage Returns: - Debt funds use changes to the bond portfolios' maturity profile or credit rating to control returns. Higher exposure to long-term debt in a fund can result in significant capital gains during a rate decline and catastrophic losses during an increase in interest rates. The NAVs of funds that primarily invest in short-term securities, such as Treasury bills or money market debt, on the other hand, are stable and do not yield capital gains. Having AAA or AA+ debt on the credit side guarantees principal protection, but it is likely to result in the lowest yields. While a greater exposure to bonds with lower ratings may result in higher coupon income, it also raises credit risk.Therefore, in order to control risk and provide exceptional returns, the top-performing debt funds must make astute and thoroughly considered decisions regarding interest rates and credit.

Who should invest in debt funds: -

Investors seeking Consistent income: Risk-averse investors, such as retirees, seeking steady income, should consider debt funds that invest in high-quality bonds or maintain short durations.

Investors who are conservative or new to mutual funds: Investors who are conservative or new to mutual funds and do not want to assume the risk of investing in equity funds may want to consider corporate bond funds or short duration funds as an alternative to bank fixed deposits. The debt fund investment is likely to yield higher returns in addition to liquidity and withdrawal flexibility, particularly in a declining interest rate environment.

Investors seeking to buy stocks during a bear market: Combining a debt fund and a Systematic Transfer Plan (STP) can help even the most aggressive stock investor. In a sideways or bearish market, for instance, a STP from a debt fund to an equity fund will minimize average cost because it permits recurrent transfers from the debt fund to buy equity fund units.

Investors seeking to stashed short-term capital: Rather than putting short-term surpluses in a bank account, households and businesses can use them to fund liquid or ultra-short duration funds. Even household emergency funds can be held in an overnight or liquid fund and earn a small return. An FMP is an option for investors who have a set investment horizon.

Consider below before investing: -

While debt funds are considered to be among the least risky mutual funds, investors should remember that they are still products of the market, just like all other mutual funds. Even the top-performing debt funds are subject to interest rate and credit risk, and returns cannot be guaranteed. Fund managers have limited control over market interest rates, which determine interest rate risk. Months' worth of capital gains can be lost by an unanticipated rate increase, particularly for a long-duration fund.

The possibility of principal and interest payment default by the bonds held by the debt fund gives rise to credit risk. It is evident from the IL&FS downgrade and the ensuing value erosion for certain debt funds that even liquid assets are susceptible to the negative effects of credit default. By closely examining the fund's parameters, choosing the top-performing funds with a track record, and ensuring that their expectations for risk and return match the debt fund's investment goal, investors can reduce risk.

Taxation: -

Debt funds offer investors the possibility of capital gains and dividends. The difference between the purchase price and the redemption or sale price of units is known as a capital gain.

The period of time an investor owns units in a mutual fund determines how capital gains are taxed. Capital gains on redemption or sale are regarded as short-term capital gains and are subject to taxation at the investor's applicable income tax slab rate if the investor remains invested in the debt fund for less than one year.

However, the debt fund is regarded as a long-term capital gain , if it is redeemed or sold after being held for more than one year. This means that before determining the capital gain, the purchase price is raised to account for inflation (using a government-provided index). Currently, the rate of taxation on long-term capital gains is 20%.

Treasury Bills

Risk Category: Treasury bills are often seen as a lower-risk (but lower-reward) investment than other debt securities, despite the fact that interest rates and inflation can affect them. The government's whole faith and credit are supported by Treasury notes. T-bills are regarded as almost risk-free investments if kept until maturity.

An instrument for the money market, Treasury Bills are issued by the Indian government. The bill is presented as a future-repayment promissory note. Securing money to satisfy the government's short-term funding needs is the goal of a treasury note. The goal is to reduce the nation's budget deficit.

These are three-period investment instruments that have 91, 182, and 364 days as their durations. A subscriber can ultimately make a profit by redeeming a treasury bill at nominal value, which is initially issued at a discounted rate.

When redeemed at face value, Treasury bills, commonly referred to as T-bills, enable the subscriber to realize a profit on their investment. Let's use an example involving Treasury bills to clarify:

Let's say you purchase several INR 150 treasury bill units at a discounted rate of INR 145. You can redeem it at INR 150 when it matures to receive INR 4 in profit for each unit.

The RBI issues the Treasury bills as part of its open market operations. To regulate the total money supply, these bills are typically issued during a time of economic expansion and high or ongoing inflation. Hence, reducing the sharp price increases that have an impact on the nation's poorest regions.

T Bills types and maturities: -

Let's examine the various kinds of treasury bills now that we are aware of their meaning.

There are three kinds of T-bills. The maturity period of Treasury bills defines these types. Currently, you can purchase Treasury bills for the following terms:

Treasury bill due in 91 days

Treasury bill due in 182 days

Treasury bill due in 364 days

T- Bill Yield Calculation: -

Treasury bills yield guaranteed returns, as previously stated. The annual return on your investment is computed using a T-bill yield. Put differently, given an investment of Rs. 100 and a profit of 5 INR over 91 days, what would be your annual profit at this rate?

Having said that, the following formula can be used to determine the T-bill return:

Yield = [Discount Value]/ [Bond Price] * [365/number of days to maturity]

Calculating T-bill yield according to this formula,

Yield = [5/100] * [365/ 91]

= 20.05%

Taxation: -

According to the income tax slab rate they are in, a subscriber would have to pay short-term capital gains on Treasury bills. On the other hand, TDS is not due from the retail investor at redemption.

Purchasing T-Bills

Now that you are familiar with the fundamentals of T-bills, let's concentrate on how to buy them. Through the establishment of a "Retail Direct Scheme Account" with the RBI, retail investors in India can purchase Treasury bills, or T-bills. Additionally, Treasury bills are available for purchase on stock exchanges, in primary and secondary markets.

Through the Reserve Bank of India: To purchase Treasury bills, an investor must first create an online Retail Direct Gift Account (RDG) with the RBI. You can make transactions from your savings account by connecting these accounts to it. Treasury bills are available for purchase through periodic auctions conducted by the RBI.

Through Primary and Secondary Markets: The stock exchange is a means of purchasing government securities. You'll need a Demat account for this. Any bank or broker can be used to open a Demat account. The investor can start trading government and private securities as soon as the account is set up.

Treasury Bill characteristics

1. **Zero-Coupon Securities:** Unlike other investment options, Treasury bills do not provide you with an interest rate. Rather, these are zero-coupon securities that provide returns via the price differential, or the difference between the selling price and the discounted rate.
2. **Minimum Investment:** In order to obtain a short-term Treasury bill, an individual must invest a minimum of INR 25,000, per RBI regulations. The person may only invest in multiples of Rs 25,000 if they would like to exceed this minimum amount.
3. **Guaranteed Returns:** Treasury bills provide returns that are guaranteed. The investor always receives a return on their investment because they are always redeemed at face value, even when they are purchased at a discount.

Government Treasury Bill Benefits

The following are benefits of purchasing Treasury bills:

1. **No Market Risk:** The performance of the market affects the returns on investments made in stocks and other investment schemes that include them. When the market is doing well, you will make a lot of money; when it is not, you could lose money. Treasury bills, or T-bills, on the other hand, have fixed returns. This implies that even in instances where the market underperforms, your returns will be assured. When Treasury

notes are purchased at a discount and sold for face value, profits will be made.

2. **They are Highly Liquid:** When the Treasury Bill maturity period ends, you can quickly turn your holdings into cash because Treasury notes are also readily available for purchase on the secondary market.

Treasury Bill's limitations

For investors who want to limit their exposure to risk, Treasury bills are an excellent choice. They do, however, have a unique set of drawbacks:

1. **Low Returns:** Treasury bills offer modest returns despite being a safe investment. The returns are negligible compared to other investment options, and they may not assist you in achieving your financial objectives.
2. **Taxes:** Treasury bill returns are liable to STCG tax. They will be subject to taxes based on the investor's tax slab rate.
3. **Affected by Inflation:** Inflation may have an effect on the returns received on Treasury Bills. When the rate of return is less than the rate of inflation, it takes place.

What Determines the Price of T-Bills?

The following variables affect returns and prices on T-bills:

1. **Market Risk:** With regard to other categories of government securities, market risk stems from the unfavorable fluctuations in the securities' values as a result of shifts in interest rates. Losses in valuation are the outcome. Treasury bills, on the other hand, don't provide investor interest. They do promise returns as a result of the discounted issuance of Treasury Bills.
2. **Inflation:** The returns on your Treasury bills may be impacted by inflation. For instance, your investment in government security may be worthless if the inflation rate is 6% and you receive a return using a 3% discount rate.
3. **Government Funding Requirements:** The government issues Treasury bills in order to raise the funds necessary to meet their immediate needs. As a result, the funding requirement and the RBI's monetary policies affect the price of T-bills.

Example of Treasury Bill Purchase: -

You can better grasp how treasury bills operate by looking at this example of one:

Suppose you invest in T Bills which are issued at a discount and redeemed at the face value at maturity. For example, a 91 day Treasury bill of Rs,100/- (face value) may be issued at say Rs.98.20, that is, at a discount of say, Rs.1.80 and would be redeemed at the face value of Rs.100/-.

Bonds

Risk Category: Corporate, government, government agency, and municipal bonds are the four broad groups into which most bonds fall. Risk considerations: Credit risk, interest rate risk, and market risk are the main risks connected to corporate bonds.

Investors purchase bonds as financial instruments in order to earn interest. Purchasing a bond is essentially lending money to the issuer, which could be a business or a government agency. The bond has an interest rate and a predefined maturity date. On this maturity date, the issuer agrees to return the principal, or the total amount borrowed. Additionally, the issuer normally pays the investor interest at prearranged intervals, usually semiannually, during the period leading up to maturity.

Typically, bonds have two uses in your portfolio. Initially, they offer a consistent and predictable source of income in the form of monthly interest payments. They are therefore appealing to people seeking steady returns. Secondly, they aid in portfolio diversification. Because bonds and stocks usually have a negative correlation, they can be used to offset potential losses from riskier investments.

Types of Bonds

There are many different types of bonds, each with their own advantages and characteristics; with so many options, it's critical to comprehend the sometimes subtle but significant differences among the most common types. Bonds are a symbol of stability and security in the world of finance.

i) Corporate Bonds: -

Fixed-income securities known as "corporate bonds" are issued by businesses to fund their expansions or operations. When purchasing these bonds, individual or institutional investors decide to lend money to the business in return for principal repayment at maturity and interest payments (the bond coupon). Corporate bonds have a wide range of risk and return, which typically reflects the creditworthiness of the issuing company. Because of this, doing research before making an investment is crucial.

ii) Treasury Bonds

Government issues Treasury bonds as long-term investments. Their maturity spans are 10, 20, or 30 years. Because the government is backing these bonds, they are thought to be extremely safe. They offer lower yields than other bond types because of their low risk. But the prices of these longer-term, lower-yielding bonds can quickly come under pressure when market interest increases. Treasury bonds are a safe, long-term investment option for investors.

iii) International Government Bonds

Debt instruments issued by foreign governments are known as international government bonds. They give investors the chance to geographically diversify their portfolios and possibly profit from yield increases or currency fluctuations. They can carry additional risks, such as exchange rate volatility and political unpredictability, depending on the nation or area, which makes them a riskier option for investments.

iv) Municipal Bonds

States, cities, or counties may issue municipal bonds, sometimes known as "munis," as a means of raising money for public works projects or operations. They can offer investors a consistent cash flow of interest, just like other kinds of bonds. Furthermore, these bonds usually have tax benefits because the interest earned is often free from central, state, and local taxes.

v) Green Bonds

Debt instruments known as "green bonds" are sold to raise money for green initiatives like reducing pollution or using renewable energy. In addition to earning interest, this enables investors to support sustainability. Similar to ordinary bonds, but with money set aside for environmentally friendly projects. Although they provide a means of making ethical investments, it is crucial to make sure that they are not just greenwashing but are really supporting projects that have a positive ecological impact.

Points to consider before investing in Bonds: -

When investing in bonds, it's important to take into account maturity dates, which specify when you'll get your principal back, interest rates, which impact bond prices and yield, and credit ratings, which show the issuer's capacity to repay debt. Making sure you comprehend these crucial elements will greatly assist you in making wise choices and coordinating your bond investments with your overall financial objectives. Additionally, remember that there is an inverse relationship between bond yields and prices. Yields decrease when bond prices rise, and vice versa. This is because a bond's fixed interest payment increases in value relative to the market when prices decline, thereby raising the yield. On the other hand, the yield decreases if bond prices rise because the fixed interest payment becomes less appealing.

How to Purchase Bonds

There are two primary options available to purchase bond securities: bond funds or individual bonds.

Individual Bonds

One can purchase individual bonds directly from the issuer, through brokers, or through banks. Nevertheless, private investors are not able to purchase certain individual bond securities. The following are a few explanations for this:

a) High minimum purchase: A significant initial investment is necessary for some bonds, which is typically beyond the means of individual investors.

b) Restricted accessibility: Some bonds are not easily found on the retail market, particularly those that are exotic or foreign.

c) Regulation limitations: Institutional investors may only be able to purchase some bonds, such as corporate or municipal bonds.

Bond Funds

In contrast, bond funds, which function similarly to mutual funds or bond exchange-traded funds (ETFs), aggregate the capital of numerous investors in order to purchase a diverse range of bonds. Although there are recurring fees, this offers the opportunity for increased diversification and expert management. Depending on your desired level of involvement, risk tolerance, investment goals, and desired exposure, you can choose between individual securities and bond funds.

Bond securities are available for either holding or active trading. The strategies of holding and trading bonds are different. Purchasing bonds and holding them until they mature ensures a principal return, barring issuer default. Conversely, trading bonds entails purchasing and disposing of bonds prior to their maturity with the intention of capitalizing on changes in value. That said, there's a greater risk involved.

Summary:

Every type of bond, whether corporate, municipal, or government, has distinct qualities that affect the risk and return profile of the investment. Prior to making an investment, it is essential to comprehend the differences between them as well as the connection between bond securities' prices and market interest rates. This can assist in confirming that the bonds you have chosen fit your risk tolerance and financial objectives.

National Saving Certificates (NSC)

Risk Category: Because NSC investments are supported by the Indian government, they are essentially risk-free. Among fixed income instruments, these investments have one of the good rate of return.

You can open a fixed-income investment plan called a National Savings Certificate (NSC) with any post office branch. The Government of India launched this initiative to encourage users, who are primarily low- to mid-income investors, to save money on investments and income taxes. You can open a joint account with another adult or invest in NSC in your name, on behalf of a minor, or from the closest post office. The five-year NSC has a set maturity period. The amount of NSCs that can be purchased has no upper limit.

Eligibility to invest in NSC

Investing in NSC is a safe option for anyone seeking to reduce their tax liability and earn a consistent rate of return on their investment. NSC provides total capital protection along with interest guarantees. But like most fixed income plans, they can't beat inflation with returns comparable to the National Pension System and tax-advantaged mutual funds.

The National Savings Certificate is a personal savings plan that has been pushed by the government. Thus, trusts and Hindu Undivided Families (HUFs) are not permitted to invest in it. Moreover, NSC certificates are not even available for purchase by non-resident Indians (NRI). The program is only available to individual Indian citizens.

The requirements listed below must be fulfilled in order to be eligible to invest in NSCs.-

1. Investments in NSC are prohibited for Hindu Undivided Families (HUFs), Trusts, and Private and Public Limited Companies (PLCs).

2. The individual needs to be a citizen of India. It is not permissible for Non-Resident Indians (NRIs) to invest in NSC.

3. There is no upper or lower age limit for certificate purchases.

Features & benefits of NSCs

- **Fixed income:** At the moment, investors are guaranteed a 7.7% return on their investment thanks to this scheme. Generally speaking, NSC offers higher returns than FDs.
- **Categories:** Initially, NSC VIII Issue and NSC IX Issue were the two types of certificates available under the scheme. In December 2015, the government terminated the NSC IX Issue. Thus, at this time, only the NSC VIII Issue is available for subscription.
- **Save taxes:** You are eligible to receive up to Rs. 1.5 lakh as a government-backed tax savings plan under Section 80C of the Income Tax Act, 1961.
- **Start modest:** You can make an initial investment as little as Rs. 1,000 (or multiples of Rs. 100) and increase it as needed.
- **Interest rate:** The government adjusts the interest rate every quarter, and as of Q1 FY 2023–24, it is 7.7% p.a. Annual compounding is required, but payment is due at maturity.
- **Maturity period:** Five years make up the maturity period.
- **Access:** After completing the KYC verification process and submitting the required paperwork, you can purchase this scheme from any post office. Additionally, transferring the certificate between post office branches is simple.
- **Collateral for loans:** NSC is accepted as security or collateral by banks and NBFCs for secured loans. This can be accomplished by

the concerned postmaster transferring the certificate to the bank and stamping it.

- **Compounding power:** Although the returns on your investment do not outpace inflation, the interest you earn is automatically compounded and reinvested.
  Nomination: In the sad event of the investor's passing, they can designate a family member—even a minor—to inherit it.
- **Corpus following maturity:** You will be paid the full maturity value at the time of maturity. The subscriber is responsible for paying the relevant tax on NSC payouts as there is no TDS.
- **Early withdrawal:** In general, it is not possible to leave the program early. They will, however, accept it in extraordinary circumstances, such as when an investor passes away or if a court order is in place.

Tax Benefits of NSC

The maximum amount that can be invested in NSC is unlimited, but under Section 80C of the Income Tax Act of 1961, subscribers are only eligible for tax rebates on contributions up to Rs. 1.5 lakh annually. Additionally, the interest received on the certificates qualifies for a tax break and is added back to the original investment.

In addition, the interest earned on NSC is eligible for a tax credit for the first four years, provided it is reinvested, or returned to the original investment, up to a total annual limit of 1.5 lakh. However, the interest earned in the fifth year is taxed at the investor's applicable slab rate because it is not reinvested.

How can one invest in NSC?

Physical NSC certificates were previously issued by post offices or banks. Since 2016, this has been discontinued. Currently, certificates can be purchased through Passbook mode or Electronic mode (e-mode).

An authorized bank or post office will easily allow you to purchase an NSC scheme with a savings account, even though the passbook method is less common and much more time-consuming. But, it's crucial to remember that in order to accomplish the same, you would need to activate your online banking.

The following documents must be submitted in order for investors to apply for NSC:

Identity verification documents include passports, driver's licenses, PAN cards, senior citizen IDs, and any other official government identification photo.
proof of address, such as a bank statement, phone bill, passport, or electricity bill.

How can one open an NSC at the postal service / Post Office

Go to the Post Office location closest to you.

Complete the application and send it in with the required paperwork.

Pay the NSC account with a cashier's cheque, money order or direct deposit.

Following completion of the processing, an acknowledgement will be provided.

An electronic investment in the NSC is possible if you have a savings account at a bank or post office (e-mode). Additionally, in order to invest in the NSC, you will need access to internet banking for your savings account.

How can NSC certificates be redeemed or cashed after they mature

The NSC may be cashed at any Post Office branch upon maturity; it is not required to do so at the branch where the account is maintained. In order to withdraw funds from a branch other than the one where your account is based, you will need to fill out an application that includes information about your account, including your full name, registered address, date of issue, serial number, and current address.

The following paperwork must be with you in order to cash the maturity amount:

Original NSC certificate; Identity verification; NSC encashment form; After payment, the person eligible to receive the encashment must sign behind the certificate.

What is the five-year NSC interest rate

For NSC, the maturity period is five years. There is no upper limit on the quantity of NSCs that can be acquired. One government program with a fixed return and minimal risk is the National Savings Certificate. The current interest rate in NSC is 7.7% annually.

What are the advantages of making an NSC investment

NSC provides total capital protection along with interest guarantees. But like most fixed income plans, they can't beat inflation with returns comparable to the National Pension System and tax-advantaged mutual funds. The National Savings Certificate is a personal savings plan that has been pushed by the government. Under Section 80C of the Income Tax Act, investments made in non-performing certificates (NSCs) are tax deductible up to a maximum of Rs 1.5 lakh. Despite the fact that the interest is taxable. The interest received on FDs, however, is subject to taxation based on the investor's income tax bracket. Because NSC is a low risk, fixed return investment backed by the Government of India, it is typically chosen by investors who are risk averse or who want to diversify their portfolio using a fixed return instrument.

Disadvantages to invest in NSC

Under the category of "Income from Other Sources," interest on NSC is subject to taxation. Nonetheless, interest is reinvested during the first four years and is therefore deductible under Section 80C of the ITA. The interest for the fifth year, or the final year, is taxable based on your income tax slab. Every time you choose to invest in this scheme, you would need to purchase a new certificate because it does not offer a reinvestment option. Because the offered interest rate is fixed, it might not provide real returns if inflation is higher.

Money Market Instruments

Risk Category: As they are low-risk instruments with short maturity periods, they are highly liquid. Money market instruments are usually issued by the government, banks and corporations having high credit ratings; hence, they are considered to be secure.

What is Money Market:

Short-term financial assets with a one-year liquidity period or less are traded on stock exchanges in the money market. Trading bills or securities are very liquid. Additionally, by exchanging bills, these help the participant with their short-term borrowing needs. Typically, banks, significant institutional investors, and individual investors participate in this financial market.

The money market on the NSE and BSE stock exchanges features a wide range of instruments. These consist of commercial paper, repurchase agreements, certificates of deposit, and treasury bills, among others. Investments in the money market are regarded as safe because of the high degree of liquidity of these securities.

The interest rates on different money market instruments are set by the Reserve Bank. The money market has a lower level of risk. This is due to the fact that the majority of the instruments are only a year old or younger.

As a result, there is less time for a default to happen. Thus, the money market is a market for financial instruments that are almost exact equivalents of cash.

What are Money Market Instruments

Financial instruments known as money market instruments assist businesses, corporations, and governmental organizations in raising short-term debt to meet their needs. The lenders profit from interest rates and liquidity while the borrowers get inexpensive short-term financing to meet their needs. Bonds, Treasury bills, certificates of deposit, commercial paper, etc. are examples of money market instruments.

What Benefits and Drawbacks Do Money Market Instruments Have

Benefits of Financial (Money Market) Instruments

The benefits of making investments in money market instruments are as follows:

Extremely Liquid: Compared to other fixed-income securities, money market instruments are more liquid, allowing investors to sell their holdings at any time. There is no lock-in time for these instruments.

Greater Interest Rate: Money market instruments have a marginally higher interest rate than standard savings accounts. For this reason, these are a better option than keeping cash in a savings account.

Drawbacks of Money Market Instruments

The drawback of money market instruments is as follows: Doesn't provide returns that beat inflation Money market instruments have higher interest rates than savings accounts, but this doesn't always mean that inflation and a growing economy are offset by them. Money market instruments may not be the best option, therefore, if the investment goal is capital appreciation while outpacing inflation.

Features of Financial Market Instruments

> It is a financial market that is not located in a specific place.

> It is a market for immediate financial requirements, like those for working capital.

> The Reserve Bank of India (RBI), commercial banks, financial institutions like LIC, etc., are its main participants.

> Treasury bills, commercial papers, certificate of deposits, and call money are the primary money market instruments.

> Because it contains instruments with maturities shorter than a year, it is extremely liquid.

The majority of money market instruments offer fixed rates of return.

Money Market Instrument Types in India

1. Treasury Bills

Among money market instruments, Treasury Bills are among the most widely used. Their short-term maturities are not the same. It is provided by the Indian government at a discount for a period of 14 to 364 days.

When they mature, these instruments are repaid at par after being issued at a discount. A company, firm, or individual may also buy TBs. 25,000 for 14 days, 91 days, and 1,000,000 for 364 days are the lots in which they are distributed.

2. Commercial Bills

Another money market instrument that functions more like the bill of exchange is commercial bills. Companies issue them to cover their immediate cash needs.

The liquidity offered by these instruments is far superior. In the event that someone needs money right away, the same can be transferred from one person to another.

3. Certificate of Deposit

Commercial banks accept Certificates of Deposit (CDs), which are negotiable term deposits. It is often distributed using a promissory note.

CDs can be distributed to trusts, corporations, and private individuals. Scheduled commercial banks can also issue the CDs at a discount. And they last anywhere from three months to a year. When provided by a financial institution, the same is valid for a maximum of three years and a minimum of one year.

4. Commercial Papers

In order to cover their immediate working capital needs, commercial paper corporations (CPs) issue CPs. therefore acts as a substitute for taking out a bank loan. Additionally, commercial paper has a duration of one year to fifteen days.

The Reserve Bank of India establishes the guidelines pertaining to the CP issue. Therefore, in order for a company to issue a CP in the market, RBI approval is required beforehand. Moreover, CP must be distributed at a price lower than face value. The discount rate is also determined by the market.

Denomination and CP's dimensions:

Minimum amount: 25 lakhs rupees

100% of the issuer's working capital is the maximum size.

5. Call Money

This is a market niche where scheduled commercial banks make quick loans or borrowings (let's say for a 14-day period). in order to oversee daily financial flows.

Because the market determines interest rates, supply and demand have a significant impact on them. Additionally, historically, there have been periods when interest rates have fluctuated significantly.

Money Market Funds

Money Market Mutual Funds, also known as MMMFs, are extremely liquid open-ended funds that are typically utilized for emergency situations. The money market fund exclusively deals in fixed income instruments with an average maturity of one year, including cash and cash equivalents.

The money market instruments that the fund manager invests in include bills of exchange, commercial paper, certificates of deposits, and treasury bills.

Who should Invest in Mutual Funds for Money Markets

For investors with a short investment horizon, money market mutual funds are a safe and appropriate option. The low risk associated with these mutual funds' money market instruments sets them apart.

Money market mutual funds (MFs) aim to maximize returns by investing across a variety of money market instruments, resulting in a diversified portfolio.

Thus, money market mutual funds are an excellent option for investors seeking a short-term, highly liquid, and secure investment.

Market Linked Investments

These days, a growing number of investors are searching for strategies to take advantage of market opportunities while lowering their risk. Market-Linked Investments could offer an answer. With market-linked debt instruments, investors can adjust their risk and return profiles and apply market perspectives in ways that may not be possible with conventional stocks, bonds, and managed funds. Put simply, they are debt securities, or bonds, whose value is contingent upon the performance of one or more other assets. Market-Linked Investments are issued for fixed terms, like one to five years, and are still subject to issuer credit risk, just like other corporate bonds. Market-Linked Investments give you exposure to the performance of a market index, a single stock, commodities, foreign exchange, or interest rates rather than paying you a traditional interest coupon. Market-Linked Investments can be bought on the secondary market or through a new issue offering.

Let's understand few market linked instruments popular in Indian Market:-

Unit Linked Insurance Plan (ULIP)

Risk Category: the investments made are subject to risks associated with the capital markets. This investment risk in the investment portfolio is borne by the policyholder. Thus, you should make your investment choice after considering your risk appetite and needs.

The full name of this multifaceted life insurance product is Unit Linked Insurance Plan, or ULIP. A ULIP plan combines investment and life insurance. As a policyholder, you must pay regular premiums to ULIPs; a portion of these payments is used to fund life insurance coverage. The remainder is combined with the assets received from other policyholders and used to invest, much like mutual funds, in financial instruments (i.e., debt and equity). Investing in ULIP allows you to grow your money while protecting it from unexpected losses.

Learn more about ULIP plans, including what they are and how to invest in them.

ULIP Plan: Advantages

What are the benefits of a ULIP plan, you ask? ULIP refers to the chance to make long-term investment returns by investing in a variety of market-related securities, including debt, equity, and balanced funds. Unit Linked Insurance Plans, or ULIPs for short, are financial plans where your investments are based on market conditions. Hence, based on your risk tolerance and financial goals, you can use the ULIP plan to invest in a range of fund options.

The following are additional advantages of ULIP plans:

- **Market linked Returns**
  With ULIPs, investors can allocate a portion of their premium to market-linked instruments, such as debt and equity instruments, in varying proportions, thereby taking advantage of the opportunity to earn market-linked returns.

- **Savings and Life Protection**

  Unit linked Insurance Plans (ULIP full form) not only allocate a portion of the premium invested into market-linked instruments, but they also assist in safeguarding you and your loved ones against life's unexpected events.

  As a result, you can benefit from market-linked returns while having your protection needs met by the ULIP plan. After taking care of your need for protection against unforeseen events, you can use ULIP plans to establish a consistent saving and investing routine and gradually accumulate significant wealth.

- **Flexibility**

  Unit Linked Insurance Plans, or ULIPs for short, give you the flexibility to switch between investment funds in response to changing needs, which helps you reach your financial goals.

  Take partial withdrawals once the initial five-year lock-in period has ended.

  Single premium additions to enable you to invest extra funds as needed in addition to the regular premium.

- **Level Payment of Premiums**

  All regular premium or limited-term premium payments made under a ULIP plan must follow a consistent, level premium payment structure. All subsequent premium payments are considered a single premium in order to offer life insurance coverage.

- **Even Distribution of charges**

  In order to help guarantee that the insurers do away with the large upfront costs, IRDAI claims that the fees assessed on ULIP plans are dispersed equally over the course of the 5-year lock-in period. Before you invest any money, make sure you are aware of the costs associated with the ULIP plan.

- **Tax Advantages**

  Under Section 80C of the Income Tax Act of 1961, the premium paid towards ULIP plans is deductible from taxes up to a maximum of Rs. 1.5 lakh. In addition, under Section 10(10D) of the Income Tax Act of 1961, the maturity/death benefit received under the ULIP plan is free from taxes.

How Do I Pick the Best Plan for ULIP

The next step is to select the best policy for you out of the many options available after you have a better understanding of what a ULIP plan is. Thus, you should think about comparing and evaluating to select the best ULIP plan available in India before you invest in a ULIP plan. The following are some essential considerations for selecting the top ULIP plan:

i) Assess Your Objectives
ii) Pick the Appropriate Level of Life Insurance Coverage
iii) Maintain Your Investment for a Long Time
iv) Get Maximum Tax Benefits Under Sections 10 and 80C (10D)

Which Type of Investors Are ULIPs Best Suitable For

1) **Those who desire to keep a close eye on their investments**

As the policyholder, you can keep a close eye on your portfolio with a ULIP plan. These people can also take advantage of the switching flexibility provided by ULIP plans, which allows them to change the capital allocation between fund options that have different risk-return profiles. Having ULIP gives you greater control over your financial planning, including choices about investments and insurance.

1) **Those with an extended to medium-term investment horizon**

If you are willing to stick with your investments for extended periods of time, the ULIP plan is perfect for you.

2) **People with Different Risk Profiles**

A range of fund options, each with a different risk return profile, are available through ULIP plans. Therefore, in order to maintain realistic return expectations, investors with varying risk profiles—from those who are risk averse to those who have a healthy appetite for risk—must be aware of the ULIP plan funds that are available before making an investment.

3) **Investors at Every Life Stage**
   You can safeguard yourself and your loved ones against monetary demands and liabilities at particular times by choosing from a variety of ULIP plan types.

Fund Options to invest under ULIP

Among the most popular investment choices offered by ULIP plans are:

a) Equity Funds

The designated investment amount in an equity fund of ULIP plans is used to buy stocks, each of which has a Net Asset Value (or NAV) attached to it. The cost per share, or "unit," in a fund is known as NAV. Because the ULIP plan is a market-linked instrument, as suggested by its full form, investing in equity carries a high inherent risk due to market fluctuations. Equity investments, though, may also yield the highest returns.

b) Debt Securities

Debentures and government bonds, which carry a lower risk than equity investments, are purchased with the premium allotted to debt funds. Debt funds in ULIP plans, however, might provide a lower return on investment than equity investments.

c) Balanced or hybrid funds

Hybrid or balanced funds are intended to offer lower risk (because of the debt component) and capital growth (from the equity component) under ULIP plans. Therefore, any loss you experience from the equity portion of the fund is offset by the lower risk but steady returns from the debt portion of the fund in the event of market fluctuations.

Making wise decisions will be made possible by having a thorough understanding of what ULIP plans are and your investing goals.

Structure plan of ULIPs

The Unit Linked Investment Plan, or ULIP plan, offers investment options that are structured similarly to mutual funds.

Investments from various investors are pooled in ULIP plans and then distributed to various fund options according to personal preferences.

ULIP plan assets are overseen by committed fund managers whose primary goal is to achieve predetermined investment goals. As an investor, you have the option to purchase shares, or "units," in a single strategy or to distribute your funds among a number of market-linked ULIP funds.

You have to make an initial lump sum payment if you decide to invest in a ULIP fund. You must then pay the plan's premiums on an annual, semi-annual, or monthly basis. The estimates generated by the ULIP calculator clearly show that the premium payment obligation differs between ULIP plans. A designated investment mandate is proportionately funded with the premium paid into a ULIP plan.

ULIP, on the other hand, offers investors flexibility by letting them change their fund preferences at any point during the investment period, based on their needs.

How does ULIP works

When you pay a premium for a Unit Linked Insurance Plan (ULIP; full form: Unit Linked Insurance Plan), the insurance company deducts certain charges, and the remaining amount is allocated to the funds of your choice.

1) Charges for fund allocation

2) Fees for policy administration

3) Fees for fund management

4) Death Penalties

ULIP is a long-term financial plan that offers numerous opportunities for wealth creation. However, the purpose of the ULIP as a life insurance product is to offer more varied returns in the form of protection from life insurance.

The insurance company appoints professional fund managers to oversee the investments under ULIP plans. Therefore, you don't have to keep track of the investments yourself. To maximize profits and manage market volatility, you can, if you'd like, monitor the performance of each ULIP plan fund option and switch between funds (at no additional cost).

Mutual Funds

Risk Category: Mutual fund investments are subject to market risk , read offer document carefully before investing. (Mutual fund category wise risk explained in a separate chapter)

Mutual funds can be considered market-linked investments in the sense that their performance is directly influenced by the performance of the underlying securities in which they invest. These underlying securities can include stocks, bonds, money market instruments, or a combination thereof.

Here's how mutual funds are market-linked:

- **Stock Market Performance:** The success of the stock market has a direct bearing on mutual funds that invest mostly in equities. Investors may benefit when the stock market rises because the mutual fund's holdings' values usually climb along with it. On the other hand, in the event of a collapse in the stock market, investors may incur losses due to a decline in the value of the mutual fund's holdings.
- **Bond Market Performance:** Changes in the bond market have an impact on mutual funds that hold bonds. Bond prices and, by extension, the value of bond mutual funds can be impacted by various factors, including shifts in interest rates, the credit quality of bonds, and general economic conditions.
- **Market Risk:** Mutual funds are exposed to a range of market hazards, one of which is market risk, which is the possibility of suffering losses as a result of shifts in the general state of the market. Additional risks include those associated with the particular securities in which the fund invests, including currency, interest rate, equity, and credit risk.
- **Diversification:** To reduce some risks, mutual funds frequently try to spread their assets over a range of markets, industries, and asset classes. Diversification can help spread risk, but it does not completely remove the possibility that changes in the market will have an impact on the fund's overall performance.

- **Active v/s Passive Management:** Mutual funds can be either passively managed (index funds), which seek to mimic the performance of a certain market index, or actively managed (portfolio managers make investment decisions in an effort to beat the market). Market conditions still affect mutual funds that are active as well as those that are passive.

Overall, while mutual funds provide investors with the opportunity to participate in the financial markets and potentially earn returns, they also expose investors to market risks. Investors should carefully consider their investment objectives, risk tolerance, and investment horizon before investing in mutual funds.

What exactly are Mutual Funds ?

A mutual fund is a type of investment instrument in which numerous individuals pool their funds in order to generate capital gains over time. A portfolio manager or fund manager is an expert in investments who oversees this group of funds. His or her responsibility is to invest the corpus in a variety of securities, including equities, bonds, gold, and other assets, with the goal of generating prospective returns. The investors split the investment's profits (or losses) jointly according to how much each contributed to the fund.

What are different types of Mutual Funds: -

In India, mutual funds offer a diverse range of investment options catering to various investor preferences, risk appetites, and financial goals. Here are some common types of mutual funds available in India:

1) **Equity Mutual Funds:** Your money is invested in stocks by equity funds. One of these funds' main goals is capital appreciation. However, there is an increased level of risk associated with equities funds because their returns are dependent on changes in the stock market. Because the amount of risk decreases over time, they are a suitable option if you want to invest for long-term objectives like saving for retirement or purchasing a home.
2) **Debt Mutual Funds:** Debt funds primarily allocate their investments towards fixed-income securities, including corporate and government bonds, debentures, and money market

instruments. Debt funds are a good option for investors seeking capital preservation and steady income because they carry comparatively lower risk than equity funds.

3) **Hybrid Mutual Funds:** Hybrid funds, also referred to as balanced funds, make investments in a combination of debt and equity securities. The fund's investment objective may influence how equity and debt are allocated. Hybrid funds are appropriate for individuals looking for a balanced approach to investing since they provide diversity across asset types.
4) **Index Funds:** These funds seek to mimic the performance of a certain market index, like the Sensex or Nifty 50. Since index funds use a passive investment approach, their expense ratios are usually lower than those of actively managed funds.
5) **Sector Funds:** Investing in stocks of businesses in a particular industry or sector, like banking, healthcare, or technology, is the main emphasis of sector funds. Compared to broad equity funds, sector funds may be more volatile but offer targeted exposure to specific industries.
6) **Tax saving Mutual Funds (ELSS):** Section 80C of the Income Tax Act provides tax incentives for mutual funds called Equity Linked Savings Schemes (ELSS). ELSS funds have a three-year lock-in period and are predominantly invested in stocks.
7) **Liquid Funds:** Investments made by liquid funds are made in short-term money market securities with 91-day maturities. These funds are a low-risk substitute for typical savings accounts for investors looking to lodge excess funds since they offer high liquidity.
8) **Gilt Funds:** Government securities (G-secs) issued by the federal or state governments are purchased by gilt funds. Interest rate risk exists, however the credit risk associated with these funds is minimal. Those who have a cautious attitude for risk can consider investing in gilt funds.
9) **International Funds:** These funds make investments in foreign markets, giving Indian investors access to international bonds, stocks, and other assets. International funds provide chances to profit from growth in the world economy as well as diversification benefits.

In this section we will explain in detail about Equity and Debt Mutual Funds:

1) **Equity Mutual Funds: -** Equity funds, as their name implies, make investments in the stock of various companies. The fund manager distributes his investments among businesses in various industries or with varied market capitalizations in an attempt to provide high returns. These funds typically have higher returns than debt-based funds or term deposits. These funds come with some risk because their performance is dependent on different market situations.

Features of an Equity Mutual Fund

An equity mutual fund will typically carry the below-mentioned characteristics:

Returns: Among all mutual funds, equity mutual funds have some of the highest returns. These funds have the highest return rates since they are invested in stocks.

Tax Benefits: Investing in these funds can provide tax advantages for you. When you sell the units of your stock fund that you have held for more than a year, you realize long-term capital gains. These capital gains are tax-free up to Rs 1 lakh annually. Over this threshold, any long-term capital gains are subject to 10% LTCG tax (no indexation advantage).

Risk: The equity funds have a high level of risk. Because stocks make up the majority of its investments, this fund is very sensitive to changes in the market.

Expense Ratio: Because these funds require ongoing administration, their expenditure ratios are typically greater than those of their competitors.

Long-Term Investments: Given their strong long-term performance, these funds are appropriate for investors with a lengthy investment horizon.

Types of Equity Mutual Funds

There are various ways of categorizing equity funds. Here is a look at the different categorizations:

Based on Investment Strategy, Classification

Thematic or Sectoral Funds: An equity fund may choose to focus on a particular theme of investing, such as developing markets or foreign stocks. Additionally, several schemes may allocate funds to specific industry segments such as BFSI, IT, pharmaceuticals, etc. Here, it's crucial to remember that because sector- or topic-based funds concentrate on a certain area or issue, they are riskier.

Focused Equity Fund: This fund makes investments in up to 30 equities of businesses whose market capitalization was defined at the scheme's inception.

Contra Equity Fund: These funds, as their name implies, invest contrary to conventional wisdom. These investment strategies search the market for undervalued equities, which are then bought at a discount with the expectation that they would eventually rise in value.

Categorization based on Market Capitalization

Certain schemes may choose to invest exclusively in businesses with a given market capitalization. These are typical types:

Large Cap Funds: A subset of equity funds known as large cap funds allocate a significant amount of their assets under management (AUM) to equity shares of highly capitalized businesses like Reliance, HUL, TCS, and others. These businesses are well-known in the industry for having a solid reputation.

Mid Cap Funds: An equity mutual fund type known as "mid-cap funds" invests in the shares of mid-sized businesses, defined as those with market caps of at least Rs.5,000 crore but less than Rs. 20,000 crore. Generally speaking, mid-cap companies are those that are ranked between 101 and 250 on the basis of their market capitalization.

Small Cap Funds: A business is often categorized as a small cap firm if its market capitalization is less than Rs. 5,000 crore. Small cap funds are funds that specialize in making investments in these kinds of small cap companies. Listed on the Indian stock markets are small-cap market companies such as Bajaj Consumer Care, Shobha Ltd, and VST Industries.

Multi Cap Funds: Mutual funds that invest in large-, mid-, and small-cap equities, among other market capitalizations, are known as multi-cap funds. Fund managers are able to adjust to shifting market conditions thanks to this broad strategy, proactively distributing assets according to opportunities that are now there. A multi-cap fund is thought to be a superior choice for building wealth since its fund managers may take advantage of investing opportunities all around the market. Additionally, any investor can locate a Multi Cap program that aligns with their budget.

Large and Mid Cap Funds: which typically allocate about 35% of their total assets to large-cap firms and 65% to equity shares of mid-cap enterprises. These schemes combine better returns with less volatility in an excellent way.

How does an Equity Mutual Fund works:

If a mutual fund scheme invests more than 60% of its total assets in the equity shares of various companies, it is categorized as an equity mutual fund. Depending on the scheme's investment goal, the remaining sum may be invested in debt securities or money market instruments.

Additionally, the fund manager has the option to allocate funds in a value- or growth-oriented manner and chose companies based on his evaluation of which investments will yield the highest returns.

How to and who should Invest in Equity Mutual Funds:

Before making any investing decisions, you should carefully consider your risk tolerance, investment horizon, and financial goals. To facilitate comprehension, we have separated the investors into two main groups: novice investors and experienced investors.

Novice Investors: Many novice investors are hesitant to enter the capital market because they lack the necessary funds, the necessary time to continuously monitor their investments (which is essential when purchasing shares), or the necessary experience to select the appropriate shares. They therefore use equities mutual funds. It might still be difficult to choose the best equity fund, though, because there are numerous varieties accessible. Therefore, while investing in these funds, it is best to choose them after taking your investment horizon, risk tolerance, and market conditions into account.

Experienced Investors: If you're an experienced investor, you may already be familiar with the performance of these funds. To reduce risks, though, apply your knowledge well before making an investment. Your knowledge of the market can assist you in selecting the best scheme and outperforming other funds in terms of returns.

What Makes Equity Mutual Fund Investments the Best Choice?

Compared to other low-risk funds, return percentages on equity funds are higher. It offers a great chance to diversify your portfolio and help you build money.

In addition, these mutual funds offer numerous other benefits, such beating economic growth, protecting against inflation, surpassing fixed-return investment plans, and much more.

In order to achieve your Retirement goals, equity mutual funds are the ideal choice because they provide the highest returns over the long run (three years and beyond).

2) **Debt Mutual Funds:** - A debt fund is a kind of mutual fund scheme that makes investments in money market instruments, corporate debt securities, government bonds, and other fixed-income assets. These funds are ideal for investors looking for a comparatively steady and predictable source of income because they are professionally managed by asset management companies (AMCs).

   Debt funds are renowned for their liquidity, which makes it simple for investors to acquire and sell units. They also provide diversification across a variety of debt instruments, which helps reduce risk.

   Debt funds are a flexible option for a range of investment goals and risk profiles because their returns are derived from interest income and capital appreciation, and their taxes is contingent upon the length of the holding term. These funds are sometimes referred to as bond funds or income funds.

How Debt Fund Works ?

Debt funds use your money to invest in different types of debt securities, like government or corporate bonds. They purchase these instruments at a discounted price and then sell them on margin at a later date. The difference between the instrument's purchase and sale prices influences the fund's net asset value (NAV).

NAV appreciates when selling prices are more than buying prices; NAV depreciates when selling prices are less than buying prices.

They get interest on their debt investments on a regular basis, much like with bank savings accounts. The fund receives these interest revenues, which raises the NAV.

The credit rating and interest rate of the underlying assets have an impact on the net asset value (NAV) of the debt funds. A bond's price fluctuates along with market interest rates.

For instance, a decline in market interest rates typically translates into lower yearly interest rates for newly issued bonds. To further grasp this, let's look at an example:

Let's say that your fund has been allocated to a debt instrument with an 8% yearly interest rate. However, they may now receive 6% yearly interest due to a decline in the market interest rate. The 8% bonds' price might rise as a result of this adjustment to reflect the return on bonds with lower interest rates. Consequently, the fund's NAV rises in tandem with an increase in the bond's price.

Who should invest in Debt Funds ?

To guarantee steady returns, debt funds often diversify among a range of instruments. The returns are often within the projected range, but there are no guarantees. Therefore, they are perfect for low-risk investors. Both medium- and short-term investors can benefit from these funds. If you want to invest in debt funds and protect your money while still earning higher post-tax returns than fixed-rate bonds (FDs), then this is a suitable alternative. It's a smart choice if you want to achieve your short-term objectives.

Debt funds are quickly redeemable and highly liquid; redemption requests are typically fulfilled in one or two working days. There is no lock-in period, as contrast to bank fixed deposits or recurring deposits. With mutual funds, there are often no penalties for withdrawing an investment early, however certain funds may have a minor exit load.

The overall expense ratio of a debt fund cannot be greater than 2% of assets under management, per SEBI regulations. Debt funds that are liquid and overnight have very low expense ratios, whereas funds that are dynamic and long-term have higher ratios.

Debt funds for Retirement:

Debt funds are better suited for short-term goals, it's true, but some of you aren't ready to take the chance. Those investors might think about investing in debt funds because, in contrast to equities funds, they carry less risk and are more stable. But if you have time horizon for your retirement on a longer side, you must choose investing through equity mutual funds for building your retirement corpus. Over time, the asset class known as equities performs significantly better than both inflation and fixed income securities. Therefore, it is advised that he invest in equity mutual funds rather than debt funds in order to increase his retirement corpus. Your monthly investable excess might be divided evenly among SIPs of different equity mutual funds that are advised.

Systematic Investment Plan (SIP)

Instead of making a lump-sum investment, a Systematic Investment Plan (SIP) allows you to invest a fixed amount in a Mutual Fund scheme at regular intervals, such as once a month or once a quarter. The installment amount, which is similar to a recurring deposit, could be as low as INR 500 per month. It's convenient because you can instruct your bank to debit the amount every month.

SIP has grown in popularity among Indian mutual fund investors because it allows them to invest in a disciplined manner without having to worry about market volatility or market timing. Mutual Funds' Systematic Investment Plans are by far the best way to get started in the world of long-term investing. It is critical to invest for the long term, which means you should begin investing early in order to maximize your overall returns. To get the most out of your investments, your mantra should be "Start Early, Invest Regularly."

A systematic investment plan, also known as a SIP, is a method of investing in mutual funds in which an investor selects a mutual fund scheme and invests in it at regular intervals. An SIP investment plan works by investing a small amount of money over time rather than a large sum of money all at once, which could result in higher returns.

How does a SIP work?

When you enroll in a systematic investment plan, the funds are automatically deducted from your bank account and reinvested in a mutual fund that you purchase at predetermined intervals. By the end of the day, you will have been assigned mutual fund units based on their net asset value.

With each SIP plan investment in India, any additional units will be added to your account at the market rate. With each investment, the amount that you reinvest will be greater, in addition to any returns that you see on those investments. The investor chooses whether to receive the returns at the end of the SIP's tenure or at any other time. Let's look at an example to help us understand this better.

Assume you want to put your money into a mutual fund of your choice. As a result, you set aside one lakh rupees to invest in the same. There are two ways to go about making this investment. You can either make a one-time payment of one lakh rupees into the mutual fund of your choice, known as a lump sum investment. You can also invest through a systematic investment plan (SIP). The procedure will be as follows:

- Begin by deciding how much you want to invest each month through your SIP. Let's say you choose Rs. 500.
- Following that, Rs. 500 will be deducted from your account each month and automatically credited into the mutual fund (as units) in which you wish to invest on a monthly basis.
- This process will continue for the duration of your systematic investment plan that you have chosen.

Types of Systematic Investment Plans:

The following are the various types of systematic investment plans in which you can consider investing:

- **Top-up SIP:** This type of systematic investment plan allows you to increase your investment amount on a regular basis while also allowing you to invest more when you have more money to invest. This type of SIP also assists one in making the most of their investments by investing in the best and highest performing funds at regular intervals.
- **Flexible SIP:** As the name implies, this type of systematic investment plan allows you to choose the amount you want to invest in. The amount to be invested can be increased or decreased based on an investor's cash flow and needs or preferences.
- **Perpetual SIP:** This type of SIP Plan allows you to invest without regard to when the mandate expires. A systematic investment plan typically has an end date after one, three, or five years of investing. As a result, the investor has the option to withdraw the amount invested regardless of whether he wishes to invest in accordance with his financial objectives.

Benefits of SIP investing:

Here are some of the numerous advantages of investing in a SIP rather than a lump sum investment. Some examples are provided below: -

Makes you a more disciplined investor:

If you lack superior financial knowledge about how the market moves, a SIP can be an excellent investment option. You do not need to spend time analyzing market movements to determine the best time to invest in something. Your money is automatically deducted from your linked bank account and invested in mutual funds when you set up a SIP.

Rupee cost averaging: -

Rupee cost averaging is one of the most significant benefits of SIPs. Because the amount invested remains constant over time, rupee cost averaging allows you to take advantage of market volatility. Because you have chosen a fixed amount to invest, your SIP will average out the value of each unit. As a result, you can choose to buy more units when the market is low and fewer units when the market is high. In the end, this will reduce your average cost per unit.

Power of Compounding:

SIPs allow the small amount you invest on a daily basis to grow into a large corpus as a sum of your contributions with compounded returns over time. SIPs have a distinct advantage over traditional investment options due to the power of compounding without the hassle of having to invest a lump sum amount.

How Do I Select a Good Mutual Fund SIP ?

The answer lies in determining why you are investing and what your goal is. If you have a long-term goal in mind, such as saving for your child's higher education, marriage, or a dream home, you should select a mutual fund SIP that allows you to invest over time. A SIP for short-term investment goals, such as home renovations or vacations, would be one with a short investment horizon.

Before deciding on a SIP, you should also consider the fund's expense ratio. The expense ratio is the annual percentage charge required to manage or operate your investment portfolio. This varies by fund, with

SEBI-mandated ceilings for equity and debt schemes, as well as on the basis of net assets.

When selecting a good mutual fund for SIP investment, consider the fund philosophy, investment horizon, and your own goals. Also, rather than focusing on a nice mutual fund for SIP, consider which fund best fits your investment principles and timeframe. There is no such thing as the best; only what is best for you, and no two people choose the same fund.

Considerations to make when choosing your SIP frequency

SIPs can be monthly, quarterly, weekly, or daily. You might be perplexed about the SIP interval you should choose. You can base your decision on your income, expenses, ongoing EMIs, investment scheme, financial goals, and so on. However, when deciding how frequently you want to invest in a specific SIP, you should consider the following factors and their impact on the SIP frequency.

The impact of volatility

The frequency of your SIP should be determined by the volatility of the investment avenue. If the volatility of your mutual fund or stock SIP is high, you can invest in a higher frequency SIP to benefit from market volatility by averaging out your investment over time, and vice versa.

Your cash inflows' frequency

If you are a salaried professional with a monthly income, it is best to invest in a monthly SIP. If you work on a contract basis and receive income every few months (for example, in the construction industry or interior design), you can choose to invest in a SIP on a quarterly basis. When you earn on a fortnightly or weekly basis (for example, internship, task completion, etc.), you can plan to invest in weekly SIPs.

Summary:

SIPs are effective tools for investing in the stock market, particularly for middle-class salaried investors. However, before you invest in a SIP, make sure you have a basic understanding of both the stock market and the fund managers' strategies.

FAQs

What is SIP Mutual Fund meaning ?

Systematic Investment Plan is the full form of SIP in mutual funds. It is a type of mutual fund investment route in which an investor can invest a set amount of money in a mutual fund scheme at regular intervals (usually monthly).

How does SIP Investment works ?

When you invest in a SIP, your money is invested at regular intervals in the mutual fund scheme of your choice. Each investment is treated as a separate transaction, and you receive units based on the scheme's current net asset value (NAV). The cumulative value of your investments grows over time as the value of the units increases.

What is the minimum investment for SIP ?

The minimum SIP investment varies depending on the mutual fund scheme. It can range from as little as Rs. 100 to as much as Rs. 500 or more.

How often can I invest in SIP ?

Most mutual fund schemes allow for monthly SIP investments. Some schemes also provide SIP options on a quarterly or biannual basis.

Can I Stop or pause my SIP Investment ?

Yes, you can pause or discontinue your SIP investment at any time. Most mutual fund companies let you do this via their online portal or by contacting customer service.

How do I choose the right mutual fund scheme for SIP Investment ?

When selecting a mutual fund scheme for SIP investment, consider factors such as the fund's track record, the fund manager's experience, the fund's investment objective, and your investment goals and risk tolerance.

Mutual Fund Risk Categories

Mutual funds have some level of risk, just like any other type of investment vehicle. It's important to consider these risks before making an investment. Generally, an investor's risk tolerance is taken into consideration when making investing selections. A person may choose risk-averse fixed-income investments in their retirement years, whereas someone in their early or mid-20s may invest more aggressively in stocks. The underlying portfolio assets of the mutual fund scheme determine the risk. Consequently, instead of being displayed at the category level, the risk is now at the fund level.

One of the first things you'll notice when you open a scheme-related document is a semicircle with an arrow pointing to the fund's "Risk" levels. The "Riskometer" was introduced by SEBI in 2015 as a risk benchmark for the specific plan. Before then, fund companies would designate low, medium, and high risk, respectively, using the colors blue, yellow, and brown. However, the granular hazards connected to mutual fund schemes were not captured by the riskometer that was established at the time. In order to identify and categorize risk under low, low to moderate, moderate, moderately high, high, and very high risk depending on their respective categories, SEBI further developed it.

The master circular recognized market capitalization, volatility, and liquidity in the riskometer and calculated risk based on the real underlying holdings of a fund. Over time, it has proven to be effective in encouraging investor openness on both the debt and equity sides.

Mutual fund companies utilize the riskometer, a standardized method, to convey the risk levels of various funds. It provides a graphic depiction of a fund's risk profile, with varying risk levels represented by a needle (much like a compass needle):

Low Risk: Principal is expected to be subject to Low Risk for investors in funds designated as "Low Risk." This category of investments is appropriate for those who are prepared to assume low levels of risk.

Moderately Low Risk: Investors who place money in funds designated as "Low to Moderate Risk" should anticipate a low level of market risk to their principal. Those who invest cautiously should consider this group.

Moderate Risk: As the name implies, "Moderate Risk" funds are appropriate for investors who lean toward conservatism but are nonetheless willing to take calculated chances with their money in the hopes of making a profit.

Moderately High Risk: The invested principle in schemes falling under this category is usually subject to equity-oriented risk. Aggressive investors with a medium-to long-term investment horizon (three years or more) should consider these.

High Risk: "High Risk" plans are appropriate for risk-takers who are prepared to commit to long-term investments (>5 years). Principal invested in these schemes may be more volatile in the market and at high risk.

Very High Risk: Compared to the extremely volatile stocks of other funds, these schemes primarily invest in equity with a higher relative risk profile. For really active investors, it is appropriate. With the aim of creating long-term wealth, the invested principle is exposed to the highest risk in this mutual fund. The funds in this category include small, midcap, international, sectoral, and theme funds.

Investors can better understand the risks involved in mutual fund investment by using the Riskometer, which serves as a useful tool. Investors can make well-informed judgments and effectively manage risks to reach their financial goals by being familiar with the categories of the Riskometer and matching them with their comfort levels, goals, and investment durations.

For example, ultra short-term funds (those with a maturity duration of fewer than 90 days) and gilt funds are generally associated with minimal risk. Risk-averse investors looking for a consistent income stream with low-risk, low-return growth may find these products appealing because of their comparatively low risk-to-return benefit. However, for long-term objectives like retirement or a child's college education, investors with a significantly larger risk appetite, the patience to wait, and the willingness to stay in the market for the long haul might think about investing in high-risk funds.

Those who are planning for goals like vacation, a lifestyle improvement, etc., may want to pick moderately high-risk funds because they typically invest in large market capitalization companies or multi-cap funds, which provide investors the option to choose between large-cap, mid-cap, or small-cap companies. Large chances for medium- to long-term investing are presented by moderate-risk funds, which are appropriate for investors who can commit to a two- to three-year investment period and who are seeking moderate earnings at the expense of a low degree of risk.

Investors can use the new riskometer as one of the criteria to choose mutual funds that match their risk tolerance levels, given the wide range of options available. Investors looking to compare the fund's risk profile to their own can benefit from this indicator.

But it's important to keep in mind that, even while the riskometer can give an overview of the risk level, it can't be the only factor taken into account when choosing a fund to invest in. When choosing a fund, there are a number of additional things to take into account, like your investment goal, your time horizon, the fund's past performance, etc.

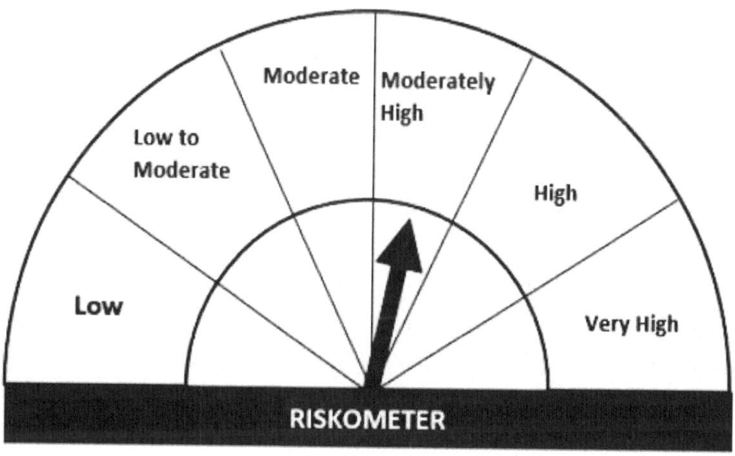

How to Use Annuities to Meet Your Retirement Income Needs

When a member of the National Pension System (NPS) retires, he or she must use at least 40% of the accumulated corpus to purchase an annuity. Previously, a subscriber could only purchase one annuity from an annuity service provider. However, the Pension Fund

Pension Regulatory and Development Authority (PFRDA) recently changed the rules. If the subscriber has a corpus of more than Rs. 10 lacs, he can purchase multiple annuities (each annuity scheme must be worth at least Rs. 5 lacs).

Multiple annuity plans must be purchased from the same annuity service provider (basically an insurance company). This rule change places the onus on NPS subscribers to select annuities wisely to meet their retirement income needs.

How does an annuity plan work? The annuity purchaser pays a lump sum to the insurance company, which guarantees the purchaser an income stream for life based on the current interest rate.

At the moment, it is unclear whether all multiple annuities must be purchased at the same time or whether the NPS will allow subscribers to stagger purchases. Annuities' returns improve with age. If, for example, the rate of return is 6% at the age of 60, it could theoretically increase to 6.5% at the age of 65, 7% at the age of 70, and so on. Subscribers should buy annuities at regular intervals if the NPS allows staggered purchases. If staggering is not permitted, subscribers should purchase an immediate annuity when they retire, and then purchase deferred annuities that begin paying out at the ages of 65,70,75, and so on.

Investors can deal with inflation by purchasing deferred annuities. Assume you have a Rs. 5 crore corpus at the age of 60. You will need Rs.50,000 per month to cover your post-retirement expenses. If the annuity rate is 6%, you can invest Rs. 1 crore and generate an annual income of Rs. 6 lacs.

However, after five years, Rs.50,000 per month may no longer be sufficient. Your monthly requirements could rise to Rs.75000. In other words, you'll need an extra Rs.25000 per month. You can then invest another Rs.50 lacs at a 6% rate to generate an additional Rs.3 lacs per year. However, if you get a higher rate of return on your investment, you may need to invest less.

There are several annuity options available, and subscribers should understand how to choose the one that is best for them. The with-return of purchase price annuity is one option, and the without return of purchase price annuity is another. The original invested amount is returned to the subscriber's nominee after the purchaser (or the purchaser and his spouse, depending on the option selected) dies.

The invested amount does not return to the subscriber's nominees in the absence of a Return of premium option. The advantage of such plans, however, is that they provide a higher rate of return than the return of purchase price option. By selecting this option, a person can generate a comparable income stream while investing a smaller sum. This frees up funds for other financial objectives. The disadvantage of the option with no return of purchase price is that if the subscriber and his spouse die before the annuity matures, the money invested in the annuity is lost. This option is preferable for people who want to earn a higher income with a small corpus or who do not have dependents.

Your health status should also influence whether you purchase an annuity with or without a return of purchase price. Someone who is in poor health should select the with return of purchase price option.

An annuity is a payment option that is made as long as the purchaser is alive. There are also options in which the annuity continues to be paid to the spouse after the subscriber's death. This is an essential feature for those who are married and have a financially dependent spouse. Thus, when purchasing an annuity, the buyer should carefully consider all of the options available and make an informed decision.

Post Office Monthly Income Scheme

The post office depository service offers a wide range of schemes with fixed returns on investment. These schemes are all backed by the sovereign guarantee, implying that this investment avenue is government-backed. As a result, when compared to equity shares and many fixed-income options, these schemes are safer investment options.

With an interest rate of 7.4%, the Post Office Monthly Income Scheme, among others such as the Post Office Savings Account, Post Office Recurring Deposit, and Post Office Time Deposit, is one of the highest-earning schemes. The interest in this scheme is paid out monthly, as the name implies. The Ministry of Finance recognizes and validates this scheme, as well as other post office schemes.

Features of Post Office Monthly Income Scheme: -

Lock in Period: - You cannot withdraw the amount deposited in a Monthly Income Scheme account before 5 years if you open one with a post office.

Maximum limit: - The scheme allows for a maximum investment of Rs. 9 lakhs. Even if you have the scheme in multiple post offices, the total amount of your deposits cannot exceed Rs. 9 lakhs. In the case of joint accounts, your share of the investment should also be within the specified limit. Minor accounts have a maximum limit of Rs. 3 lac. For any individual, the minimum amount that can be invested is Rs.1500/-.

Transferable: If your residential status changes to another city in India, you can transfer your POMIS account to a nearby post office. Your investment corpus and interest disbursement from the Post Office Monthly Income Scheme will be carried forward to such a post office.

Joint account: This scheme allows a maximum of three people to open a joint account. In the case of joint accounts, each investor has equal access to the funds. In the case of joint accounts, the maximum limit is Rs. 15 lakhs, and the singular limit is Rs. 9 lakhs.

Minor account: You can open a POMIS minor account in your child's name. Minors under the Post Office Monthly Income Scheme must be over the age of ten. He or she can withdraw the amount after 18 years of maturation.

Eligible residential status: While every Indian citizen is eligible to open a POMIS account, NRIs are not.

Auto-withdrawal: You have the option of withdrawing the monthly interest on your investment via automatic transfer to your savings account via PDCs or ECS. If the POMIS account is associated with a CBS Post Office. The interest earned can then be transferred to any other CBS-related savings account.

Penalty: If you wish to withdraw your investment corpus before the lock-in period expires, you will be charged a penalty based on the time of redemption.

Investment amount: Any amount in multiples of Rs. 100 is permitted as an investment.

Tax advantages: The interest amount does not incur any Tax Deducted at Source (TDS), but it also does not qualify for any tax advantages under Section 80C.

The maximum investment limit for the Post Office Monthly Income Scheme is shown in the table below: -

ACCOUNT TYPE	MAXIMUM LIMIT
Single Account	Rs.9 lac
Joint Account	Rs.15 lac
Minor Account	Rs.3 lac

Required documentation:-

Copy of government-issued ID proof, such as a passport, voter ID card, driving license, or Adhaar card.

Address verification: a government-issued ID card or the most recent utility bill.

Photographs: - One passport-sized photograph.

Procedure for Opening a POMIS Account: -

It is simple and painless to open a Post Office Monthly Income Scheme Account (MIS). To invest in the scheme, however, you must have a Post

Office Savings Account. If you haven't already opened a savings account with the Post Office, you can use the following procedure –

1. Get a POMIS Form from your local post office.
2. Submit the form with the following documents: a photocopy of your ID, a photocopy of your address proof, and two passport-sized photographs.
3. Submit the originals of the above-mentioned documents for verification.
4. Collect witnesses' or beneficiaries' signatures:

A dated cheque can be used to invest the capital amount. The account opening date will be the date specified on the cheque. The interest earned on the investment will be paid out one month after the investment is opened.

After opening the Post Office Monthly Income Scheme in India account, the beneficiary can also be nominated.

Eligibility for the MIS Scheme at the Post Office: -

- A resident Indian can only open a POMIS account; this system does not apply to non-resident Indians.
- Anyone over the age of 18 is eligible to open an account.
- You can open an account on behalf of a minor aged 10 or older. Children will be able to access the fund once they reach the age of 18.
- When a minor reaches the age of majority, he must apply for conversion of the account in his name.

Penalty for Early Withdrawal

1) Before the end of one year = no benefits
2) From one to three years: the entire deposit is refunded, less a 2% penalty.
3) From the fourth to the fifth year: The entire corpus is refunded, less a 1% penalty.

Post Office Monthly Income Scheme (MIS) Advantages: -

Investing in POMIS has two major advantages. It is a go-to option for many investors with a low-risk appetite because it is not a market-linked investment scheme and is guaranteed by the government. These advantages are as follows:

1. Consistent returns: You would earn a consistent monthly income from your investment corpus regardless of market fluctuations. The post office has set an interest rate of 7.70% per year.
2. Reinvestment: You can choose to reinvest your interest earnings in high-profit-yielding securities such as equity shares or equity funds; however, these investment options are also much riskier. When compared to equity shares and funds, hybrid funds, which include both equity funds and fixed income instruments, are a viable option for participating in the stock market, developing a diverse investment portfolio, earning comparatively higher returns, and taking lower risk.

Health Insurance

One of the most significant aspects of your life is your health, so it is in your best interest to have insurance that will protect you in the event that you experience any health-related problems. One such financial product that can cover the costs if you or a member of your family experiences a medical emergency is health insurance. In today's world, where medical costs are rising and healthcare has become expensive, health insurance is a crucial investment.

What is Health Insurance?

A type of insurance called health insurance offers financial support for the cost of medical care and treatments. It is a contract between the insured and the insurance provider, whereby the insured pays a premium in return for the insurance provider's assurance that it will pay for the insured person's or persons' medical expenses.

A health insurance plan gives you security during difficult times and gives you access to high-quality medical care.

Check out the features and coverage of the health insurance plans offered by different companies (based on the policy terms and conditions) now that you may have a better understanding of what health insurance is.

coverage for hospitalization costs both before and after

coverage for boarding costs, room rent, and medical expenses

Fees for medical consultations

hospital fees

Network hospitals offer the option of cashless claims (the number of cashless network hospitals varies from company to company).

There are numerous customized health insurance plans available to meet a variety of needs, including those of individuals, families, senior citizens, pregnant women, people with critical illnesses, and others.

Types of Health Insurance

Are you interested in learning more about the various types of health insurance policies and how they differ from one another? Here is a brief description of the various types of health insurance policies that are offered on the market, each with its own features and advantages, so you can pick the one that best suits you.

1) Individual Health Insurance

Hospitalization, medical costs, and treatments are covered by this kind of health insurance policy for a single person. People who are at least 18 years old are covered. It comes with a lifetime renewal option and offers sum insured options from INR 1.5 lakhs to INR 50 lakhs. Based on the insured's age, health status, and medical history, the premium for an individual health insurance policy is determined.

2) Health Guard Family Floater Plan

The entire family is covered by a single policy under this family floater health insurance. These family plans offer SI (Sum Insured) options between 1.5 lakhs and 50 lakhs INR. Extended coverage options for policies are available for up to three years. Age, health status, and medical history of the family members covered by the policy are taken into account when calculating the premium for a family floater health insurance policy.

3) Critical Illness Insurance

A type of health insurance called "critical illness insurance" covers particular critical illnesses like cancer, heart attacks, strokes, and kidney failure. When a critical illness is diagnosed, the insurance policy pays a lump sum that can be used to pay for lost wages and medical costs.

Now that you are aware of what health insurance is and the various types of plans that are available, let's examine the advantages that come with having health insurance.

Benefits of Health Insurance

The following are some advantages of the health insurance plans provided by various companies (depending on the policy choice, but generally speaking):-

a) Financial Protection

The financial support that health insurance offers for medical costs and procedures can help you budget your spending and ease your financial burden. Maximum coverage is offered by our health insurance policies at very affordable premium rates.

b) Exceptional Medical Care

You have access to high-quality medical care and treatments with our health insurance, which can guarantee that you get the best care possible.

c) Peace of mind

Knowing that you and your family are covered against the financial effects of medical emergencies gives you and your family peace of mind.

d) Simple claim resolution

The majority of businesses provide 24/7 call support for claims resolution. Additionally, for quicker and more effective claim settlement, the majority of businesses have their own in-house Health Administration Team (HAT) or Third Party Administrator (TPA).

e) Tax Advantages

According to Section 80D of the Income Tax Act, tax benefits are available for the health insurance premium paid.

Be aware that tax benefits can change if the law on taxes changes.

Additionally, you can purchase and renew health insurance online, saving you a ton of time and the hassles of complicated paperwork (but you need to check on terms and conditions carefully as no advisor is involved for online purchase) .

What is Long-Term Health Insurance ?

You ought to be aware of another type of health insurance. However, it is the tenure of the policy rather than the extent of coverage that sets it apart from other types. Do you have any questions? Let us assist.

In India, the shortest duration of health insurance is one year. However, purchasing a health insurance policy for a longer period of time is an option. By extending the duration of your insurance plan for up to 3 years, you can enjoy long-term coverage and avoid the hassle of having to renew your policy each year.

How Does Health Insurance Work ?

You may now have a clear understanding of what health insurance is, as well as some of its characteristics, advantages, and other elements. Let's now examine how the idea of health insurance functions.

The basis of health insurance is risk sharing. You are required to give the insurance company regular premium payments when you buy health insurance. The insurance provider agrees to pay for your medical costs and treatments up to the amount assured in return.

You are welcome to visit any of the network hospitals connected to your health insurance plan when you require medical attention or treatment. The insurance provider will receive the hospital's bills and verify them before approving the claim.

If the claim is accepted, the insurance provider will pay the hospital directly and you won't be responsible for any out-of-pocket expenses. You will be responsible for covering the costs of the medical care if the claim is denied.

Why Do You Need Health Insurance

Knowing what health insurance is may not be sufficient; one must also understand its significance and importance in the modern world.

According to the law, having health insurance is not required in India, but it is a requirement for getting hassle-free medical care and paying for your medical expenses.

You require health insurance for the following reasons:

a) Increased Medical Costs:
When you or a loved one needs medical care, having health insurance can help you manage the costs. Even the most basic treatments are becoming unaffordable for the general public due to the sharp increase in the cost of medical procedures and medications. The financial support that health insurance offers for medical costs and procedures can help you budget your spending and ease your financial burden.

b) Safeguards Your Savings:

Without health insurance, medical costs can significantly deplete your savings. Health insurance offers financial assistance for medical costs, which can help you safeguard your investments and savings. As a result, health insurance becomes the best tool for minimizing your out-of-pocket costs and assisting you in maintaining your savings.

c) Cashless Hospitalization:

If you've heard the phrase "cashless health insurance," you might be wondering what it means. It is a benefit of health insurance where the insurer pays the hospital bills outright. Only network hospitals have access to this feature.

They guarantee that no matter where you are, you and your loved ones will receive the best medical care possible without having to pay astronomical medical bills thanks to our extensive network of hospitals across the nation.

How Do You Pick a Reputable Health Insurance Plan ?

Given the variety of options on the market, selecting the best health insurance plan can be challenging. Here are some things to take into account when selecting a quality health insurance plan:

a) **Coverage:**
   The health insurance plan's coverage is a crucial thing to think about. Make sure the plan covers all medical costs and treatments in full, including pre- and post-hospitalization costs.

b) **Network hospitals:**
   A network of hospitals in your area may be covered by the health insurance plan. Find out if this is the case. By doing this, you can make sure that getting high-quality medical care and treatment is simple.

c) **Premium: -**
   The cost of the health insurance plan's premiums should be taken into account. Make sure the premium is within your means and is reasonable.

d) **Claim Settlement Ratio:**
Before selecting a health insurance plan, look into the insurance company's claim settlement ratio. A high claim settlement ratio shows that the business has a successful track record of handling claims and offers prompt and straightforward claim resolution.

e) **Exclusions:**
Examine the health insurance plan's exclusions to learn what is not protected by the policy. Before purchasing the policy, be sure you are aware of the exclusions.

f) **Co-payment and Deductibles:**
These are the sums you must pay out-of-pocket before your insurance company begins to pay for medical expenses. Before selecting a health insurance plan, look into the co-payment and deductible amounts.

Which Plan to Buy - a Mediclaim Plan or a Critical Illness Insurance Plan ?

While both critical illness and mediclaim Insurance policies cover medical costs financially and are made to fit a variety of needs. The main variations between the two are as follows:

a) **Coverage:** Critical illness insurance plans cover certain critical illnesses like cancer, heart attack, stroke, and kidney failure, while Mediclaim plans cover hospitalization costs, medical expenses, and treatments.

b) **Payout:** Critical illness insurance plans pay a lump sum after a critical illness is diagnosed, whereas Mediclaim plans pay out the actual costs incurred.

c) **Premium:** Due to the coverage being limited to certain critical illnesses, the premium for critical illness insurance plans is typically higher than that of mediclaim plans.

d) **Exclusions:** The two plans have different exclusions, so it's important to know what each one excludes before choosing.

Please be aware that the terms "mediclaim" and "health insurance" should not be used synonymously. In order to avoid making an impulsive, ill-informed purchase, it is crucial to investigate each of these and comprehend the distinction between mediclaim and health insurance.

Purchase Health Insurance at early stage:

Purchasing health insurance at an early stage of life is a wise decision for several compelling reasons. Firstly, young adults generally enjoy better health and fewer pre-existing conditions, which can lead to lower insurance premiums. By locking in coverage early, individuals can secure lower rates and potentially save money over the long term. Additionally, health insurance provides financial protection against unforeseen medical expenses, which can arise at any age. Accidents and illnesses can happen unexpectedly, and having health insurance ensures that individuals have access to quality healthcare without facing exorbitant out-of-pocket costs.

Additionally, a lot of health insurance policies cover wellness checks, tests, and immunizations as preventative care services at no extra cost. By utilizing these preventative treatments, people can stay in the best possible health and identify any possible health problems early on, when they can be treated more easily and affordably. Frequent examinations and screenings can also assist people in forming healthy lifestyle choices and practices that can either avoid or lessen the effects of chronic illnesses in the future.

To prevent coverage gaps, early health insurance purchasing is essential. Because life is unpredictable, things can change quickly. In the event of a medical emergency, people without health insurance run the danger of being uninsured during times of unemployment or transition, which could put them in a difficult financial situation. People can guarantee ongoing coverage and prevent the possible repercussions of not having health insurance, such as medical debt or restricted access to care, by acquiring health insurance early.

In addition, some health insurance policies provide extra services and advantages like prescription medication coverage, mental health assistance, and telemedicine. These advantages can be quite helpful in preserving general health and wellbeing, particularly in stressful or uncertain circumstances. People who enroll early in a comprehensive health insurance plan will have uninterrupted access to these resources when they most need them.

Finally, getting health insurance early lays the groundwork for future financial security and planning. Having a solid health insurance coverage in place offers stability and peace of mind as people age and their health needs change. Additionally, it frees people from worrying about the possible financial strain of medical expenses so they may concentrate on other facets of their lives, including furthering their education, developing in their employment, or beginning a family.

In summary, getting health insurance early in life is a proactive move to safeguard one's physical and financial security. The advantages of enrolling in health insurance early are varied and substantial, ranging from obtaining lower rates to having access to preventative care services and avoiding coverage gaps. People may protect their health, wealth, and prospects for years to come by making health insurance a priority early in life.

What Is the Health Insurance Claim Procedure ?

Both offline and online registration for health insurance claims is possible.

Call the relevant insurance company's toll-free number to register an offline claim, and a company representative will walk you through the entire process.

You can follow the steps listed below to register an online claim:

Cashless claims: -

You must present your policy information to the network hospital in order to submit a cashless claim. When the hospital has confirmed your information, it will send the pre-authorization form to the insurance provider. This form is examined by the insurance provider, and if the claim is approved, it provides the hospital with information about the policy details and coverage. Additionally, the insurer might write the hospital a letter of inquiry requesting more information.

Reimbursement claims:

You will need to submit a reimbursement claim if you choose not to use a network hospital. In this situation, you must obtain all necessary documentation from the hospital and provide it to the insurance provider. Following a review of these supporting documents, the insurance provider will decide whether to accept or reject the claim. In the event that it discovers that some of the required documents are missing, it will notify you and start the claim procedure once you have sent the necessary documentation.

Additionally, you have the option of selecting multiple health insurance policies and registering your claim under each one.

Summary

We hope this section has clarified what health insurance is and why it is important for you to understand. To ensure that you and your family are covered in the event of a medical emergency, we advise that you obtain a suitable policy after conducting careful research and comparisons.

Life Insurance

Insurance Planning is an integral part of any Retirement plan and without the security of insurance the retirement plan of an individual can get spoiled in case of an unexpected loss. Retirement planning includes insurance portfolio of self or family.

Life insurance is an essential financial tool that offers your loved ones comfort and safety in the case of your passing. It provides financial assistance to pay for living expenses, debt repayment, burial fees, and other charges. It acts as a safety net. Life insurance serves the fundamental function of paying out a death benefit, but it can also provide a number of other features and benefits, which makes it a flexible and important asset in your financial plan. Life insurance plans cover not only the risk of dying but also that of living long.

Life insurance is a type of financial policy that gives people and their loved ones a sense of security and comfort. Fundamentally, life insurance is a contract that an insurance policyholder signs with an insurance company, agreeing to the insurer's payment of a certain amount of money to a selected beneficiary in the event of the insured person's death. The purpose of this financial protection is to lessen the potential financial burden that the insured's passing may have on heirs or dependents. Life insurance is a centuries-old idea that originated in benevolent organizations that pooled money to support the families of their members who had passed away in ancient Rome and China. Life insurance developed into the structured policies we see today over time, providing a variety of benefits and coverage options catered to the requirements of contemporary families and individuals.

Risk management is one of the core ideas of life insurance. People can transfer the risk of financial difficulties upon their death to an insurance firm by making periodic, small premium payments. Many people find life insurance to be a reasonable and accessible kind of protection because of this risk pooling, which enables insurers to distribute the financial burden over a sizable policy holder base. Term life, whole life, and universal life insurance are the three types of life insurance plans available. Each offers unique features and benefits to accommodate a range of financial objectives and situations. Term life insurance offers coverage for a predetermined amount of time, usually between 10 and 30 years, and pays out a death benefit to the beneficiary in the event that the insured passes away during that time. On the other hand, whole life insurance offers coverage for the insured's whole lifetime and has a growing cash value component. Because universal life insurance has adjustable rates and death payouts, policyholders can modify their coverage and savings amount to accommodate shifting financial requirements.

Life insurance can be used as a tool for wealth accumulation and estate planning in addition to offering financial security. Over time, the cash value component of permanent life insurance plans can grow tax-deferred, giving policyholders access to a source of funds through loans or withdrawals under the policy. You can utilize this cash value to cover unforeseen bills, pay for education, or supplement retirement income. Furthermore, when paid to the recipient, life insurance proceeds are typically not taxable, making it a cost-effective means of passing money on to future generations. People can make sure that their loved ones are financially supported even after they pass away by including life insurance in their overall financial plan.

Life insurance can offer emotional peace of mind in addition to financial protection. It helps people feel less stressed and anxious when they think about their mortality because they know that their loved ones will be cared for in the event of their passing. After a loved one passes away, life insurance can help families continue to live comfortably, pay off debt, and reach their long-term financial objectives. This frees them up to concentrate on their own recovery and future plans. Furthermore, life insurance helps close the generational divide by guaranteeing that the insured's legacy and beliefs endure via the opportunities and assistance given to their beneficiaries. All things considered, life insurance is essential for assisting people and families in navigating the uncertainties of life with assurance and security, guaranteeing that their loved ones will always be taken care of and protected.

How much Insurance you actually need ?

According to the most recent estimate from January 2022, life insurance penetration in India has been progressively rising, but it is still quite low when compared to markets in more industrialized nations. Industry statistics show that in 2020, India's life insurance penetration rate was approximately 2.82%, meaning that just a small portion of the country's population was covered by life insurance. (However, it's important to remember that these numbers could change based on the data source and the computation technique.)

Within the insurance sector, there is a broad belief that Indians have inadequate insurance. People who are underinsured—that is, whose insurance coverage falls short of their true needs and financial situation—are caused by a number of variables. It's possible that a large number of people are unaware of the benefits of insurance or the range of coverage options. They can undervalue the risks they take on or the possible financial fallout from unanticipated circumstances, which would cause them to forgo or use insurance insufficiently. Moreover, paying insurance premiums can be very expensive for some people and families, particularly those with conflicting financial priorities or low incomes. In order to save money now, people can decide to forgo insurance entirely or choose to have reduced coverage levels. It's possible that some people think their employer-sponsored insurance or government-funded healthcare programs provide them with sufficient coverage. These plans could, however, have exclusions or coverage gaps that leave people open to unforeseen costs. Furthermore, insurance policies can be intricate and challenging to comprehend, particularly for people with little financial knowledge or experience negotiating the insurance industry. Underinsurance may come from people finding it difficult to choose the appropriate kind and level of coverage for their requirements.

Some people could be very confident in their capacity to control risks whether it comes to investing, savings, or other strategies. These tactics can be crucial parts of a financial plan, but they could not offer enough defense against some risks, such significant medical costs or income loss from a disability. Getting insurance and making future plans can be intimidating endeavors, which makes some people put off or put off taking action. Delaying getting insurance, however, might leave people open to unforeseen circumstances that, with careful planning, could have been lessened or avoided. People's insurance requirements can change as their circumstances change, such as when they get married, have a child, buy a house, or launch a business. Underinsurance, however, can result from people underestimating their future needs or failing to modify their insurance coverage appropriately.

A multimodal strategy is needed to address underinsurance, including raising financial literacy levels, simplifying insurance products, making cheap coverage options available that are catered to specific requirements and situations, and raising awareness of the value of insurance. People can better safeguard themselves and their families against unanticipated hazards and financial hardship by taking care of these elements.

So the question we should endeavor to answer is how much insurance coverage each individual should have. We'll talk about a somewhat accurate way to determine the true need for insurance.

Human Life Value – How This Is Critical Before You Buy Life Insurance

There are a few typical mistakes that people make while buying life insurance. People can make better decisions and steer clear of potential pitfalls by being aware of these serious mistakes. When buying life insurance, neglecting to calculate the human life value (HLV) might be a serious error. HLV calculation assists people in figuring out how much life insurance to buy in order to safeguard the financial security of their dependents in the case of their passing away.

Human life value can be calculated using the human life value (HLV) technique, which takes into account their income, expenses, and future commitments. It is essential in figuring out how much life insurance is necessary to safeguard the dependents' financial security in the case of the policyholder's passing. In insurance, your age, income, future demands for money, and liabilities are all taken into account when calculating your Human Life Value. For example if you intend to work for an additional 20 years and earn Rs.5,00,000 per year, for instance, your Human Life Value may be Rs.1,00,00,000 (20 years x 5,00,000).

Here's why ignoring HLV calculation can be a costly mistake:

Inadequate Coverage: One of the primary purposes of life insurance is to replace the income of the insured individual in the event of their death. HLV calculation helps determine the amount of coverage needed to replace the income that the individual would have earned over their working years. In the absence of an HLV calculation, people can understate the amount of coverage they actually require, leaving their dependents insufficiently protected. Their loved ones can become financially vulnerable as a result and be unable to cover ongoing needs like a mortgage, schooling, and daily living expenses.

Overpaying for Coverage: On the other hand, if people decide to buy more insurance than they really need, they will end up paying more than is necessary. Paying too much for insurance can put a strain on your finances and take money away from other financial objectives like investments and savings. Based on the HLV computation, one must accept the insurance coverage they genuinely need.

Covering Debts and Expenses: Life insurance policies can also be used to pay off debts that have not been paid off, including credit card obligations, mortgages, loans, and burial costs. These monetary commitments are taken into consideration during the HLV calculation to make sure there is adequate coverage to settle them without placing a financial strain on the remaining family members.

Future Financial requirements and Goals: The HLV computation takes into account future financial requirements and goals, such as keeping up the family's standard of living, saving for retirement, and paying for children's education. The right level of life insurance coverage can be chosen by projecting these future costs, ensuring that these objectives can still be met even in the event that the insured person's income is lost.

Inflation and projected Investment Returns: To guarantee that the life insurance coverage amount stays adequate over time, the HLV calculation takes into consideration variables like inflation and projected investment returns. The coverage amount can be modified to retain its purchasing power and keep up with the growing cost of living by accounting for these factors.

Providing Financial Security: The dependents of the insured individual receive financial security and peace of mind from life insurance coverage based on the HLV calculation. It guarantees them sufficient protection and the ability to continue living at their current level even in the event of the insured person's passing.

How to calculate human life value manually: Calculating human life value manually involves estimating the economic value of an individual's life based on various factors such as their age, income, future earning potential, expenses, and other financial considerations. Here's a simplified approach to calculating human life value: --

Determine the individual's current annual income. This can include salary, bonuses, investment income, etc., in addition estimate the individual's potential future income growth based on factors like career progression, inflation, and market trends. Estimate the number of years the individual is expected to work until retirement. Multiply their annual income by the number of working years to calculate the total income over their career.

From the arrived amount deduct taxes and living expenses from the total income to account for what the individual would actually retain. Consider additional financial factors such as debts, savings, investments, and future financial obligations like education expenses for children or retirement savings. Since future income is worth less in today's terms due to inflation and the time value of money, discount the future earnings to present value using an appropriate discount rate. Sum up the present value of future earnings, adjusted for taxes, expenses, and other financial considerations. This represents the estimated economic value of the individual's life.

It is important to remember that determining the value of a human life is a complex process that requires many assumptions and approximations. Depending on the unique circumstances, inclinations, and preferences of individuals or financial professionals, many approaches and considerations may be applied. In the context of insurance planning, human life value computations are also frequently utilized to establish the right coverage amounts for life insurance plans.

Types of Life Insurance

Pure term insurance and investment-based life insurance are two distinct types of life insurance products that serve different purposes and offer different features. Let's discuss in detail:

Purpose:

Pure Term Insurance: The main purpose of term insurance is to preserve an insured's finances in the event that they pass away within a predetermined time (such as 10, 20, or 30 years). It has no savings or investing component; it only provides a pure death benefit. The primary objective of term insurance is to offer monetary stability to the beneficiaries of the insured, including dependents or family members, in the event of the insured's premature demise.

Investment based life insurance: Whole life and unit-linked insurance plans (ULIPs) are examples of investment-based life insurance, which combines life insurance coverage with an investment component. These plans not only offer a death benefit but also build up cash worth over time that policyholders can access through loans or withdrawals. In addition to the death benefit, these policies' investing component seeks to increase the policy's cash value over time. This could result in further savings or investment returns.

Premiums and Cost:

Pure Term Insurance: Because term insurance just delivers a death benefit and does not build up financial value, it usually has the lowest premiums among life insurance policies. This makes term insurance policies' prices more reasonable overall, making them an economical choice for getting large coverage amounts.

Investment based life insurance: Because investment-based life insurance policies include an investment component along with related administrative fees and charges, their premiums are often greater than those of term insurance. These policies divide the premium in half, with the remaining amount going toward the policyholder's selection of funds or investment alternatives and the insurance company's costs.

Cash Value and Returns:

Pure Term Insurance: Policies for term insurance do not gradually accrue cash value. The policy expires and no benefits are paid if the insured lives out the duration of the coverage. Term insurance serves only as a tool for risk management, offering protection against monetary losses for the duration of the policy.

Investment based life insurance: Over time, cash value is accrued by investment-based life insurance contracts, which policyholders can access or surrender for cash value. The success of the underlying investments or funds that the policyholder has chosen determines how much the cash value increases. In order to perhaps improve the accumulation of cash value and investment returns, policyholders may also choose to modify their premium payments or investment allocations.

Flexibility:

Pure Term Insurance: Term insurance products generally provide simple coverage with predetermined rates and terms of coverage. They usually don't come with extra features or investment choices, though they can provide alternatives for policy renewal or conversion to permanent insurance.

Investment based life insurance: More flexibility in premium payments, investment possibilities, and policy features is frequently available with investment-based life insurance policies. The flexibility to change investment funds, modify premium payments, and take loans or withdrawals against the policy's cash value is available to policyholders.

In summary, pure term insurance focuses solely on providing death benefit protection for a specified term at an affordable cost, while investment-based life insurance combines life insurance coverage with an investment component aimed at accumulating cash value over time. The choice between these two types of life insurance depends on individual financial goals, risk tolerance, and coverage needs.

In the next chapters we will analyze Pure Term Insurance and Investment based life insurance features, benefits , pros and cons.

Term Insurance

The "term" of a term insurance policy is the amount of time that it provides life insurance coverage. A death benefit is paid to the insured person's nominees if they pass away while the policy is still in effect.

With the exception of plans like Return on Premium, etc., a basic term insurance variant has no cash value, which means that if the insured person survives the policy's term, the policy does not return any value.

Because of the sum assured that they would receive from life insurance, your dependents would be able to maintain the same lifestyle or pay off existing debts without having to give up their dreams if you were to pass away. You can buy a term insurance policy that can provide a certain corpus to your dependents.

Why Do I Need Term Insurance?

Term insurance plans have a lot of features and advantages, but some people are still unsure of how these policies will affect them. Here are three main justifications for getting term insurance:

1) To Safeguard Your Family: - You are both the financial and emotional support for your family. You might want to contribute to your parents' retirement or the higher education of your child. Even if something were to happen to you, your family could still accomplish their goals with the payout from a term plan.

2) To Safeguard Your Assets: - Today, a lot of young people need loans to help them pay for a car or a house. Your family might have to deal with your loss, the loss of your income, and a new financial burden if something were to happen to you while you are repaying a loan. They run the risk of losing the asset if they can't pay back the loan. Your family can manage debt and safeguard your assets with the payout from a term plan.

3) To manage the risks of a new lifestyle: - We learn about the prevalence of serious conditions like cancer and heart disease as well as the rise in lifestyle diseases on a daily basis. Your term

plan may be able to provide some financial assistance as you deal with this diagnosis and accept that you will need to recover and recover.

Why You Should Buy Term Insurance?

Term insurance is a straightforward product that is simple to comprehend. The following justifies purchasing term insurance:

1) An attractively large cover with a low premium: - A term insurance policy can provide significant coverage, and the premium for such a cover would be quite reasonable. Because it provides excellent protection, such a product should be the cornerstone of one's financial portfolio.
2) Dependents' finances are safeguarded: A term plan's main objective is to safeguard the policyholder's financial dependents in the unfortunate event of the latter's passing. Financial dependents can manage expenses associated with maintaining a way of life and pursue their financial objectives thanks to the sizeable death benefit provided by a term life insurance policy. Therefore, a term insurance policy would provide the policyholder with enormous peace of mind because the financial dependents' welfare would be taken care of even in the latter's absence.
3) protect your assets: Financial dependents may be required to sell assets to raise money to cover daily expenses in the absence of the primary wage earner. For instance, to raise money, a person who is financially dependent may need to sell their home or investment portfolio. Their long-term wellbeing might suffer as a result of this. Instead, the death benefit provided by a term insurance plan can offer significant money for paying bills on a daily basis or for any other need. Thus, it is not necessary to liquidate assets that have the potential to be very valuable in the long run.
4) Riders: There are various riders that can be added to a term insurance policy. These add-ons are very helpful and can strengthen the coverage of a term insurance policy. The accelerated death benefit rider, accidental death benefit, critical illness rider, waiver of premium rider, etc. are a few of these

riders. Although adding these riders might slightly increase your premium, you might get a lot of value from them.

Benefits of buying Term Plan:

Here are some advantages of buying term insurance:

High protection at affordable prices: Because they offer a substantial cover at comparatively low premiums, life insurance policies are affordable for the majority of people. The cost of term insurance decreases the earlier in life you buy it.

The additions (Add Ons) : A critical illness or an accident may render the policyholder incapable due to unfortunate circumstances. This would affect the policyholder's ability to earn an income. In such circumstances, the policyholder's family might struggle to pay bills. Consider adding additional add-ons or riders to the term insurance plan to protect yourself from such occurrences. Examples of some of these add-ons include riders for accidental disability and critical illness insurance. If the policyholder is found to have one of the critical illnesses covered by the policy, the critical illness cover would offer a lump sum payment equal to the death benefit. The accidental disability rider will guarantee that the policyholder receives a regular monthly income for a predetermined time period equal to a specific percentage of the sum assured.

Assurance of resources: In addition to being upsetting, the death of the family's primary earner creates financial obligations. Daily expenses are protected from loss in the event of the insurer's passing thanks to life insurance. In order to help the family with their living expenses, the insurance policy's payout can be received as a lump sum or in installments.

Features of Term Insurance:

Let's examine the benefits that a term insurance policy provides:

Low entry age: - Term plans with a low entry age have a low entry age of just 18. As a result, once you reach adulthood, you can buy insurance for yourself or your loved ones.

Long-Term Defense: - Term insurance offers whole life coverage, enabling you to offer your family decades of monetary security.

Variable Cover: - Depending on your changing financial needs, you can choose to increase or decrease your sum assured with a term insurance plan.

Options for Flexible Premium Payment: - You have a choice in how you want to pay your premiums when you buy a term policy. You have the option of paying a premium annually, half-yearly, quarterly, or even monthly.

Simple to Buy: - You can purchase a term policy online in modern India within a short period of time. You can evaluate the various policy benefits and alter a plan with add-ons in accordance with your particular requirements. Once you've decided which policy you want, you can pay the premium and submit a few document scans.

Liability Defense: - A term insurance policy's payout enables your loved ones to better manage debt obligations. You can assist your family members in repaying their debts and loans by buying a term plan.

Types of Term Plan

There are many flexible term plans with extra benefits available. The following is a description of the market's most well-liked proposals and plans. Depending on your needs for insurance, you can make a choice.

Pure term insurance

A pure term plan, which pays out a fixed sum assured to the nominee in the event of the insured's passing during the policy's term, is the easiest to comprehend. Such plans make no payments if the insured person lives past the policy's expiration date. Pure term insurance premiums are primarily influenced by the insured's age, gender, smoking status, policy term, premium payment schedule, and sum assured. These are products' basic offerings, and they typically have the lowest premiums out of all the available product options.

Return of premium plans

Many customers find it difficult to accept that pure term insurance policies do not offer any money back if the insured lives to the end of the policy term. For these customers, the Return of Premium plan is quite alluring, under which all premium payments (taxes excluded) would be refunded if the insurer survived the policy term. In the event of death during the term, the nominee will receive the sum assured. These types of plans are significantly more expensive than Pure Term Plans because they guarantee benefits both on survival and on death.

Increasing sum assured plan

This plan's increase in sum assured is the exact opposite of a decreasing plan; it is typically capped at a multiple of the initial sum assured. As the benefit amount rises with each passing year, the premiums are higher than they would be under a level plan. These programs aim to increase coverage as the customer's income levels rise. Many plans offer the option to increase the sum assured yearly without additional underwriting at the time of purchase. The customer can take advantage of the revised higher sum assured by paying higher premiums each year.

Term life insurance with income protection

Term insurance is typically purchased to replace lost income. The income benefit is a feature that helps product benefits better match customer needs by ensuring that the nominee receives the desired sum assured over time. In some of these plans, a portion of the benefit is still provided as a lump sum. The fact that the plan is more tax-efficient in the nominee's hands than a lump sum-based plan is one of its main advantages. Any lump sum that is guaranteed is typically invested in an interest-bearing financial instrument, and the periodic interest that is earned may be subject to taxation. Additionally, the nominee has the choice to forego any future income payments in favor of a lump sum payment equal to the present value of the remaining income benefit installments.

What is Term Insurance Rider: ?

In addition to life insurance, a term insurance rider offers additional benefits. You can choose an accidental death rider or a disability rider, for instance, which provides an additional payout in the event that the policyholder is killed in an accident or becomes disabled. The majority of insurers also offer a critical illness rider. You are given a lump-sum payment when a covered critical illness is diagnosed with this add-on. The premium waiver rider, which waives off future premiums in the event that the policyholder is diagnosed with a critical illness or other eventualities specified by the plan, is the most popular term insurance rider.

How Do Term Plans Function: ?

Similar to limited life insurance policies, term plans operate. For a set period of time, they offer life insurance. You must consistently pay premiums if you want to benefit from the life insurance. Your nominee receives the promised sum assured as the policy payout in the event that you, the policyholder, pass away while the policy is in effect. You have the option to purchase riders or add-ons to improve the financial security of your family.

Who Should Buy Term Insurance?

Let's take a look at who should buy term insurance:

Parents: Parents are constantly concerned for the future of their kids. Parents can relax knowing that they have purchased term plan. They can feel secure knowing that even if something were to happen to them, their child would still be cared for financially. They never have to worry about their child giving up on their dreams because they have a financial safety net.

Young Employees: A term plan is an option for young professionals without many debts, such as a car loan or a personal loan EMI. They make sure that their parents and other loved ones have the resources necessary to cover their debts in the event of their passing. They also gain from lower premiums, which will be beneficial in the long run.

Newly-weds: Recent newlywed couples can gain from a term plan. When their spouse most needs it, the insurance will help them financially. For young couples who want to achieve financial independence, a term plan is an essential component of any sound financial strategy.

Working Women: Today's young women sit in boardrooms and handle their finances as well. Many take on the role of the sole provider and provide financial support for their family members. These women can safeguard their parents', spouses', and kids' financial futures with a term plan. The payout from such a policy might assist in paying off any unpaid debts or even assist their loved ones in achieving their future financial objectives.

Taxpayers: Certain advantages provided by term insurance policies enable taxpayers to lower their tax obligations. Section 80C of the Income

Tax Act of 1961 permits deductions for premiums paid for term insurance policies.

Retirees: To enjoy a secure retirement, people work their entire lives. In your golden years, having a term insurance plan gives your spouse financial security. If something were to happen to you, the payout from the insurance policy would enable them to continue living as they do even without a reliable source of income.

When should you purchase a Term Insurance Plan: ?

The best time to purchase a term insurance policy is now. Since they pose very little risk, young people in good health can obtain higher sum assured amounts at lower premiums. As you age, health problems could arise that would raise your premium or lower the maximum amount of insurance you are eligible for.

How long should the Term Insurance policy period be: ?

You have the option of choosing a tenure as short as five years or lifetime coverage when you buy a term plan. In a perfect world, you would pick a plan that expires just before you retire. Payments from term insurance assist you in covering debts, the majority of which you would have paid off by the time you retire. Before the term of the policy expires, you can change the term policy into a full-life plan if you'd like to keep receiving life insurance coverage.

How to select the best Term Insurance Plan: ?

To ensure you make the right choice , you should:

Look at the claim settlement ratio: You can determine the likelihood of an insurance company settling your nominee's claim by looking at their Individual Death Claim Settlement Ratio. The Individual Death Claim Settlement Ratio of a business can be found online.

Understand the customer experience: Find out from reliable sources what they thought of the insurance provider of your choice. You may also read customer reviews on the internet to find out if people have a positive or negative experience with the business. Recall that you may have a term plan that lasts the remainder of your life, so you should establish a strong rapport with the business.

Check the solvency ratio: A company's capacity to pay its insurance obligations is shown by its solvency ratio. All insurance businesses are required by the IRDAI to have a ratio of at least 1.5. Companies' solvency ratios are available for viewing online.

Consider the benefits: Plans are not created equal. Seek out policies that provide greater benefits than others. Look for policies that provide various payment and payout options along with maturity benefits.

Choose riders carefully: Term plans provide benefits beyond life insurance. You can choose riders that also cover accidental incapacity and serious illnesses. The payouts from these add-ons might significantly help you and your loved ones during a trying period by providing financial security.

Find flexible payout options: Buying a term policy usually involves having certain financial objectives in mind. The majority of term insurance policies pay nominees in full. These people frequently become overwhelmed by the big amount and are ill-equipped to handle it. Instead, you ought to think about policies that pay out on a monthly basis. Your nominee will be more capable of managing smaller monthly sums that can assist them with more pressing financial need.

Research online availability: Make sure you can reach your insurance both online and offline before making a choice. Nowadays, the majority of businesses offer 24/7 chat support on their websites so you may get prompt responses to your questions. For speedy processing, you could also search for businesses that allow online claim filing.

Features of ULIPs

Although we have discussed regarding united linked insurance plans in our investment chapter in detail , but we will discuss briefly here to check comparison with term plan and the suitability of which for our retirement planning objective.

Unit Linked Insurance Plans (ULIPs) provide policyholders with both life insurance and investment options, making them a special kind of insurance and investment hybrid. ULIPs are essentially insurance policies that combine an investment component with a life insurance component. This gives policy holders the freedom to divide their premiums among different investment funds, like debt, equity, or balanced funds, according to their financial objectives and risk tolerance. Transparency is one of the main advantages of ULIPs; policyholders can see how their investment funds are performing as well as the costs and fees involved. Because of this transparency, policyholders are better able to make educated investment decisions and modify their asset allocations over time to better suit their evolving financial goals and the state of the market. Moreover, ULIPs provide policyholders with flexibility in premium payments, giving them the choice between regular and single premium payments. They can also modify their premium amounts or transfer investment funds to better suit their investment strategy.

Moreover, ULIPs offer a number of advantages that satisfy policyholders' various requirements and preferences. The life insurance coverage that ULIPs offer, which provides financial protection to policyholders' beneficiaries in the event of the policyholder's untimely death, is one important benefit. The death benefit that ULIPs pay out might give the policyholder's dependents or family a financial safety net by giving them a way to pay for living expenses, debts, schooling, or other financial commitments. In addition, ULIPs provide policyholders with the freedom to tailor the level of life coverage to suit their unique requirements and preferences. This flexibility enables them to modify their coverage amount or sum insured at any time to account for life events like marriage, having a kid, or becoming a homeowner.

ULIPs provide long-term savings and wealth accumulation opportunities through the investment portion of the policy, in addition to life insurance coverage. The option exists for policyholders to allocate their premiums to a diverse portfolio of investment funds, comprising of stocks, bonds, money market instruments, or a mix of these. Over time, the growth of the policy's cash value is determined by the performance of these investment funds, giving policyholders the chance to accumulate money and accomplish their financial objectives, including retirement planning, funding for education, or wealth preservation. In addition, ULIPs provide tax advantages under current legislation. Premiums paid into ULIPs are deductible from taxes under Section 80C of the Income Tax Act, and the death benefit or maturity proceeds from ULIPs are tax-free under Section 10(10D), subject to certain limitations.

Notwithstanding their advantages, policyholders should be aware that ULIPs have some risks and concerns of their own. Charges and costs related to ULIPs, such as those for fund management, mortality, policy administration, and premium allocation, are one such factor to take into account as it may affect the policy's overall results. Furthermore, because the value of investment funds is liable to change dependent on market circumstances and the performance of underlying assets, the performance of ULIPs is also susceptible to market risks. Before purchasing ULIPs, policyholders should carefully examine their risk tolerance and investment goals. They should also think about speaking with a financial counselor to make sure their investment strategy is in line with their circumstances and financial goals. All things considered, ULIPs provide a complete solution—flexibility, transparency, and the possibility of long-term wealth accumulation—for people looking for life insurance coverage together with investing options.

How Do We Select the Right Insurance Policy

Term insurance is preferable to unit linked insurance plans (ULIPs) when looking at life insurance options for a number of reasons. Term insurance is a more appealing option for anyone looking for pure death benefit protection without the hassles of investing since it provides straight forward coverage at a lower cost than ULIPs. In the case of an untimely death, policyholders who purchase term insurance pay premiums for a predetermined period, usually between 10 and 30 years, in exchange for a death benefit that is paid to their beneficiaries. Because term insurance has fixed premiums and coverage amounts for the duration of the policy, it is simple to comprehend and budget for. Furthermore, term insurance offers a high coverage amount in comparison to the premium paid, enabling people to affordably secure substantial financial security for their loved ones. Term insurance does not provide investment returns or accrue cash value like ULIPs do, thus it does not carry the same risk of market changes and related costs. Term insurance is a great option for people who value providing financial security for their dependents or family members above all else, but don't want to cope with the additional complexities and expenses of investment-based insurance solutions. Furthermore, term insurance provides flexible coverage options, allowing you to adjust the period and quantity of coverage to suit your needs and preferences.

In order to expand the breadth of protection offered by the policy, policy holders may also choose to add riders or endorsements, such as riders for critical illness or accidental death benefit, to improve their coverage. Moreover, premiums paid toward the policy are tax deductible under Section 80C of the Income Tax Act, and the death benefit received by the beneficiaries is tax-free under Section 10(10D), subject to certain limitations. Term insurance gives tax benefits under the current tax rules. All things considered, term insurance offers a simple, flexible, and worry-free means of securing financial security for loved ones during uncertain times at a reasonable rate. People can make sure that their dependents or family members are financially supported in the case of their untimely death without having to deal with the additional complexity and expenses of investment-based insurance products by selecting term insurance over ULIPs.

Investing the excess money from a Unit Linked Insurance Plan (ULIP) in mutual funds and choosing term insurance over it offers a calculated approach to financial planning that optimizes returns while lowering expenses and risks. Term Insurance is a simple and affordable way to get life insurance. If the insured passes away within the designated time, beneficiaries will get a pure death payment. If people choose term insurance instead of ULIPs, which frequently have expensive fees and charges that can reduce investment returns, they can provide substantial financial protection for their loved ones at a much lower cost. Term insurance also offers policy holders freedom and transparency, enabling them to choose coverage durations and amounts to suit their requirements and preferences. People who choose term insurance over ULIPs can benefit from expert fund management, diversification, and liquidity by putting the extra money they save in mutual funds. Compared to ULIPs, mutual funds are more flexible, transparent, and have lower charges. This allows investors to choose a diverse investment portfolio that suits their risk tolerance and financial objectives.

Investors using mutual funds have access to a multitude of investment options, the knowledge of experienced fund managers, and the liquidity to modify their strategy as necessary. In general, choosing to purchase term insurance and put the remaining assets into mutual funds presents a responsible and economical method of financial planning; it offers substantial life insurance and investment options while lowering costs and optimizing long-term returns.

Investment In Capital Market

Although we have covered a variety of investment options, buying shares, also known as equity or stock, is one of the most popular choices since it can yield relatively larger returns over longer periods of time. Although mutual funds are an indirect way to invest in shares because they restrict the investor's ability to choose a specific stock, industry, etc. A lot of people want to purchase their favored stocks by directly investing in shares. Furthermore, the most popular method for novice investors to obtain experience with investments is through stock market investing.

Even though stock investing carries a significant risk, numerous studies and research projects have demonstrated that over the long term, stocks have outperformed the majority of alternative investment options. Since the 1990s till the present, stocks have provided investors with yearly returns of about 17.5% in the form of increases in share price or capital appreciation. Therefore, when compared to other investment possibilities, stocks are thought to be the most difficult yet lucrative investment. "The process of laying out money now in the expectation of erecting more money in the future," as renowned investor Warren Buffet put it.

It's critical to perform in-depth due diligence on a company's history, finances, revenue model, management, and prospects before purchasing shares. Maintaining a varied portfolio is crucial when investing in the stock market to avoid making your portfolio particularly susceptible to the volatility of a single industry. Investing should be done with a long-term outlook, with the goal of building your retirement corpus, rather than engaging in speculative activity.

You have the option to invest in primary and secondary share markets. Applying for shares through an Initial Public Offer (IPO), or public offering, is the main method of investing in the stock market. A follow-up public offer (FPO), which is issued by a firm whose shares are already trading in the secondary market, is another way to invest in the primary market. Purchasing stock exchange-listed companies' shares is another method of investing in the stock market.

You must first open an electronic 2 in 1 Demat and Trading account with any reputable depository participant (DP) in order to begin investing in the stock market. You will have the ability to make stock market investments after opening these accounts. The following paperwork must be sent to the relevant DP in order to open a trading account in order to place trades and a Demat account in order to electronically store your securities:

i) PAN Card
ii) Adhar Card
iii) Residence Proof
iv) Cancelled cheque for bank details.

Before putting money into the stock market, investors should weigh the many benefits and drawbacks of doing so. On the plus side, the possibility of large long-term profits is one of the main advantages of stock investing. Since equities have historically produced better average returns than other asset classes like bonds or cash equivalents, they are a desirable choice for retirement planning and wealth creation. Moreover, stock investments give investors the chance to become owners of profitable businesses and take part in their expansion and success through dividends and capital development. Additionally, the stock market provides liquidity, enabling investors to purchase and sell stocks with ease and speed. This gives them the freedom to modify their investment portfolio in response to shifting market conditions or individual circumstances. Additionally, stock investing offers benefits of diversification since it spreads risk and lessens the effect of the performance of any one firm or sector on the portfolio as a whole. Stocks reflect ownership in a wide range of companies across different industries and sectors. Lastly, investors can choose from a wide range of investing options in the stock market, including mutual funds, exchange-traded funds (ETFs), and individual stocks, all of which can be used to suit a variety of investment styles and methods.

But there are risks and disadvantages associated with stock market investment that investors need to be aware of. The inherent volatility of the stock market, which may cause large swings in stock values over brief periods of time, is one of the fundamental drawbacks of stock investing. It is challenging to anticipate and successfully handle market volatility, which can be caused by a variety of reasons such as economic conditions, geopolitical events, business earnings releases, and investor emotions. Moreover, there is a chance that capital will be lost while investing in stocks because stock values might drop as a result of market downturns, industry trends, or company-specific issues. Investors who sell their assets amid downturns in the market may suffer either short-term or long-term losses. Individual investors may find it difficult and time-consuming to find quality companies with solid fundamentals and growth prospects when investing in individual stocks, which calls for thorough study and analysis. Moreover, stock investing calls for self-control and patience to endure market gyrations and prevent rash decisions based on transient market movements. The stock market is also vulnerable to geopolitical and regulatory concerns, such as modifications to tax laws, rules, or policy that may have an effect on investor confidence and market performance.

In conclusion, before making an investment, investors should carefully weigh the benefits and drawbacks of stock market investing. The stock market has risks like volatility, capital loss, research requirements, emotional biases, and regulatory/geopolitical uncertainty, but it also offers the possibility of significant profits, liquidity, diversification, and accessibility. Through a comprehensive comprehension of the advantages and disadvantages of stock investing, together with a sensible approach that fits their financial objectives, risk appetite, and investment horizon, investors may adeptly navigate the stock market and attain enduring financial prosperity.

Real Estate

Retirement planning is greatly aided by real estate, which presents a number of advantages and factors that people should carefully consider before deciding on their retirement plan. The ability of real estate to produce passive income through rental properties is one of its main benefits when it comes to retirement planning. People can augment their retirement savings and ensure a consistent flow of earnings during retirement by investing in residential or commercial real estate investments. Rental income from real estate assets can assist in paying for living expenses, medical bills, and other necessities, giving retirees stability and security in their finances. In addition, long-term capital appreciation is a possibility with real estate investments because property values often rise with time as a result of things like population expansion, inflation, and housing demand. Retirees can improve their financial well-being and leave a lasting legacy for future generations by investing in real estate, which can also help them generate wealth.

Moreover, real estate investments help retirement portfolios diversify by lowering overall investment risk and raising risk-adjusted returns. Since traditional asset classes like stocks and bonds have little correlation with real estate, real estate values may not fluctuate in lockstep with the overall financial markets. People can lessen the effects of market volatility and economic downturns by adding real estate investments to their retirement portfolios, assuring a more secure and resilient investing approach. Since property values and rental revenue typically rise over time in tandem with inflationary pressures, real estate investments also serve as a hedge against inflation. People can maintain their level of living in retirement and protect their purchasing power even during times of rising prices and economic uncertainty by investing a portion of their retirement savings in real estate.

Additionally, real estate investments have tax benefits that can increase income and retirement savings. For retirees, rental income from real estate investments offers tax-efficient cash flow because it is typically taxed at a lower rate than ordinary income. Furthermore, tax deductions for things like mortgage interest, property taxes, depreciation, and operational costs can help real estate investors by lowering their overall tax burden and boosting after-tax returns on investment. Additionally, through techniques like 1031 exchanges, which let investors postpone capital gains taxes on the sale of investment properties by reinvesting the proceeds into like-kind assets, real estate investments offer tax-deferred development potential. People can increase their retirement savings and after-tax income by utilizing tax-efficient investing strategies, which will guarantee a more pleasant and secure retirement.

But while planning for retirement, it's critical to take into account the challenges and difficulties related to real estate investments. Investing in real estate involves a large initial cost, liquidity, and continuous upkeep and administration, which can be taxing for retirees, especially those with limited financial means or physical capabilities. Furthermore, local market conditions, economic trends, and legislative changes can have an impact on investment returns and cash flow, as well as real estate valuations and rental markets. Furthermore, because real estate investments are concentrated in a single asset or region, they may be less diversified than traditional asset classes. This increases their susceptibility to particular risks such property vacancies, tenant defaults, and market downturns. In addition, compared to equities and bonds, real estate investments are less liquid since it might take time to sell a property and access the proceeds, which can be difficult in times of need or when financial circumstances change. In order to ensure a balanced and diversified approach that is in line with their financial goals and circumstances, people should carefully evaluate their risk tolerance, liquidity needs, and investment objectives before including real estate assets into their retirement planning strategy.

To sum up, real estate is a crucial component of retirement planning because it provides a host of advantages such tax breaks, capital growth, diversity, inflation protection, and passive income. People can improve their long-term wealth, provide a steady income, and increase their financial security by adding real estate investments to their retirement portfolios. To guarantee a cautious and comprehensive retirement plan, it is crucial to consider the dangers and difficulties related to real estate investments, such as initial investment costs, liquidity issues, market volatility, and management obligations. A pleasant and secure retirement can be achieved by individuals who carefully weigh the benefits and drawbacks of real estate investments and who employ a diversified approach that fits their risk tolerance and financial objectives.

Real Estate Investment Trusts (REITs)

In retirement planning, Real Estate Investment Trusts (REITs) are essential since they provide special benefits and chances for investors who want to accumulate wealth, earn passive income, and secure their retirement. Publicly listed firms known as REITs hold, manage, or provide funding for income-producing real estate assets in a range of markets, including retail, commercial, industrial, and residential. The capacity of real estate investment trusts (REITs) to generate steady, dependable income in the form of dividends is one of its main advantages for retirement planning. Because REITs are compelled by law to pay out at least 90% of their taxable revenue to shareholders as dividends, income-oriented investors—including retirees—find them to be a desirable investment choice. Investors in Real Estate Investment Trusts (REITs) can obtain a consistent flow of cash flow to support their retirement funds, pay for living expenses, and offer security after they retire.

Additionally, retirement portfolio diversification is facilitated by REITs, which lower overall investment risk and improve risk-adjusted returns. To spread risk and reduce the influence of any one property or sector's performance on the portfolio as a whole, REITs invest in a diverse portfolio of real estate properties across several geographic areas, property kinds, and sectors. Furthermore, retirees can participate in the potential development and appreciation of real estate assets without the inconvenience of property ownership or management by investing in real estate through REITs, which give them access to real estate markets that may be inaccessible or unaffordable for individual investors. Moreover, because REITs are traded on open stock exchanges, investors can purchase and sell shares with ease and speed, giving them the freedom to modify their investment portfolio in response to shifting market conditions or individual circumstances.

In addition, REITs have the potential to increase in value over time due to the development of their portfolio, increased rental income, and appreciation of property values. REITs can expand into new markets, buy more properties, and take advantage of investment possibilities as the real estate industry develops and grows, which will boost shareholder wealth and asset value. In addition, advantageous demographic trends, technical developments, and economic situations that foster the demand for real estate properties—such as urbanization, population growth, and the uptake of e-commerce—may help REITs. Retirees can benefit from the possible gains in real estate markets while reducing the risks related to financing, managing, and owning real estate by making investments in REITs.

Additionally, REITs provide tax benefits that might increase income and savings for retirement. REIT dividends give retirees tax-efficient cash flow because they are usually taxed at a lower rate than ordinary income. Furthermore, through the use of techniques like like-kind exchanges, which let investors postpone paying capital gains taxes on the sale of their REIT shares by reinvesting the proceeds into other eligible real estate investments, REITs may provide tax-deferred growth potential. In addition, real estate investment trusts (REITs) have the potential to offer exposure to tax-advantaged sectors like healthcare, infrastructure, or renewable energy, which present extra tax advantages and incentives for investors. Retirees can increase their after-tax returns and retirement income by utilizing tax-efficient investing strategies, which will guarantee a more pleasant and secure retirement.

But while planning for retirement, it's critical to take into account the challenges and difficulties involved with investing in REITs. Due to their reliance on debt financing for the acquisition and operation of real estate properties, REITs are susceptible to changes in interest rates. Increasing interest rates may have an effect on REIT share prices and investor returns by raising borrowing costs and decreasing cash flow available for distributions. Furthermore, real estate values and investment performance may be impacted by market volatility, economic cycles, and regulatory changes that impact REITs. Furthermore, the stability and predictability of retirees' income may be impacted by changes in REIT dividends over time due to changes in property occupancy rates, rental rates, and property management choices. Additionally, REITs might be exposed to particular risks related to their real estate industries, like modifications to regulations, disruptions from technology, or changes in customer preferences, all of which could have an impact on investment returns and property values. Therefore, before making an investment in a REIT, retirees should carefully consider their risk tolerance, income needs, and investment goals to ensure a diversified and balanced approach to retirement planning that fits their financial circumstances and aspirations.

To sum up, real estate investment trusts (REITs) are an essential component of retirement planning, providing a variety of advantages such steady income, diversity, liquidity, capital growth, and tax benefits. Retirees can participate in the growing potential of real estate markets, access a consistent source of cash flow, and improve the security and income of their retirement by investing in REITs. To guarantee a cautious and comprehensive retirement plan, it is crucial to consider the risks and difficulties related to REIT investments, such as interest rate sensitivity, market volatility, and sector-specific risks. Retirees can maximize their retirement savings and have a comfortable and secure retirement by carefully weighing the benefits and drawbacks of REIT investments and incorporating them into a diversified investment strategy.

Succession Planning

Legacy and succession planning are not just for businesses; they are also important for people who want to make a lasting impression on the world and make sure that their personal affairs are handled smoothly when they pass away. Legacy planning is carefully evaluating the impact one wishes to have on the world, taking into account not only tangible assets like money but also intangible assets like morals, convictions, and life lessons. It begins with introspection, which asks people to consider their basic beliefs, interests, and purpose in life. People can develop a vision for their legacy that is consistent with their values and objectives by defining what matters most to them. This vision acts as a beacon of hope, directing their decisions on the use of their time, effort, and resources as well as influencing the kind of effect they wish to leave on future generations. Legacy planning also entails identifying important stakeholders, such as friends, family, coworkers, and the larger community, who will be impacted by their choices and activities. People may make sure that their intentions are recognized and understood and that their legacy accurately reflects their genuine beliefs and aspirations by having candid and open discussions with those closest to them.

Moreover, succession planning for individuals covers objectives and duties related to personal and family life in addition to financial concerns. This involves putting vital documents like advance directives, trusts, and wills on file so that, in the case of incapacity or death, a person's desires are honored. It also entails selecting dependable people to act as guardians, trustees, and executors in order to manage the division of assets and provide for dependents in accordance with their preferences. People can ease the strain on their loved ones and guarantee a seamless transition of their affairs by taking preemptive measures, giving themselves and their family peace of mind.

People can leave a legacy by their deeds, habits, and connections in addition to material possessions. This could include giving advice and mentoring to others, volunteering for causes close to their hearts, or speaking up in favor of social and environmental change. Through imparting their knowledge, abilities, and life experiences to others, people can encourage and enable the next generation to continue their work and change the world. Furthermore, people can leave a legacy of love, support, and connection that transcends material belongings and lives on long after they are gone by developing strong relationships and nurturing ties with loved ones.

In addition, succession planning for individuals include getting the following generation ready to take over and continue their legacy. This entails giving people the chance to learn, grow as people, and acquire new skills in addition to promoting moral principles like compassion, integrity, and resilience. People can make sure that their influence endures throughout time and that their ideals and vision are maintained for future generations by giving them the tools they need to build on their accomplishments and carry on their legacy.

Trusts, foundations, and charitable bequests are a few estate planning options that people can utilize to support causes they care about and make a lasting difference in the world. People can leave a meaningful legacy that lasts beyond their own lifetime and advances society by include charity in their legacy planning. People can use their wealth and power to make a positive difference and leave a lasting legacy that will help future generations, whether they do so by starting a scholarship fund, endowing a nonprofit organization, or funding research and innovation in their profession.

In summary, legacy and succession planning is a complex process that entails defining one's beliefs, objectives, and desired future state as well as taking proactive steps to guarantee the longevity of one's legacy. People can leave behind a legacy that truly captures their personality and has a significant impact on the world by thinking back on their ideals and vision, having candid conversations with loved ones, and taking proactive measures with their finances and personal affairs. People can leave a lasting impression on future generations by shaping their legacy through relationships, activities, or real assets.

Will

Writing a will provides a legal foundation for the distribution of assets and the execution of human preferences after death, making it an essential part of estate planning for individuals. A will, at its most basic, is a legal document that specifies the distribution of a person's property and assets after their death. Despite the common misconception that only the wealthy or old should write wills, everyone with assets—no matter how small—can gain from having a will in place. Lack of a will can cause issues and disagreements within the family, hold up the transfer of assets, and have unexpected effects on close ones. Writing a will is therefore a crucial step in making sure that one's last intentions are carried out and that their estate is managed in accordance with their desires.

Taking stock of one's possessions, debts, and commitments is the first step in making a will. This entails creating an exhaustive list of all bank accounts, properties owned, investments, personal effects, and other valuables. It also entails determining whose loans, mortgages, credit cards, and other financial commitments still need to be paid off. People can clearly grasp the extent of their estate and make well-informed judgments on the distribution of their assets in their will by undertaking a thorough assessment of their financial status.

Determining how these assets should be divided among beneficiaries is the next stage in the will writing process, once the assets and liabilities have been determined. This entails deciding who will inherit certain assets, how much they will get, and under what circumstances. For instance, someone could decide to leave emotional objects or family artifacts to particular family members or loved ones. In addition, they have the option to name beneficiaries to receive cash, stocks, bonds, or other assets as bequests or inheritances. Furthermore, people could choose to create trusts or place restrictions on inheritances, including making beneficiaries wait a particular amount of time or fulfill certain requirements before getting their inheritance.

Wills not only allow people to distribute their assets but also to name executors who will manage their estate and make sure their last desires are fulfilled. In addition to finding and appraising assets, executors are essential in overseeing the probate process, handling tax and debt payments, and allocating assets to recipients in accordance with the will's instructions. As a result, selecting executors who are reliable, capable, and prepared to carry out their responsibilities appropriately is crucial. Having backup executors named is also a good idea in case the principal executor is unwilling or unable to carry out their duties.

Additionally, wills give people the chance to decide critically regarding guardianship and how to care for dependents or minor children. This involves stating their preferences for their children's welfare, education, and upbringing as well as designating guardians to take care of minor children in the case of the parents' passing or incapacity. People can make sure that their children are raised by dependable people who share their values and views and that their wishes for their children's future are honored by addressing these issues in their will.

Wills can also cover other personal considerations such as funeral and burial plans, charitable bequests, and pet care provisions. People could want to leave directives on the upkeep and care of their pets, such as how their care should be provided and how much money should be set aside for their costs. In order to help causes they are passionate about or organizations that have made a significant difference in their lives, people could also decide to leave charitable gifts or bequests. Furthermore, people can want to indicate their preferences for burial or cremation, funeral rites, and what happens to their remains after they pass away.

A vital component of estate planning for individuals is creating a will, which establishes the legal parameters for asset distribution and the execution of final desires. People can make sure their ultimate desires are carried out, their possessions are divided in the way they choose, and their loved ones are taken care of by being proactive and creating a will. Writing a will enables people to take charge of their life and leave a lasting legacy for future generations, whether they are creating a basic will or a more intricate estate plan. As a result, it is never too early to begin drafting a will and make sure that your intentions are recorded and enforceable.

If one dies without making a will (called "intestate" in legal terms), his wealth is inherited by the heirs according to the inheritance laws.

What is Nomination: ?

In the context of estate planning, nomination is an essential component that enables people to name beneficiaries for particular financial assets including bank accounts, retirement accounts, and life insurance policies. This procedure comprises stating in writing who will be entitled to these assets' proceeds in the event of the person's death. By designating beneficiaries, people can avoid the drawn-out and frequently difficult probate procedure and guarantee that their assets are transferred in accordance with their intentions. By offering a simplified process for distributing assets straight to the designated beneficiaries, nomination helps to speed up the estate settlement process and give loved ones financial security on time.

Nomination also provides flexibility, as beneficiaries can be updated when circumstances change, keeping an estate plan up to date and in line with the preferences of the individual. It's crucial to remember, though, that nomination usually only pertains to financial assets and does not cover other parts of estate preparation, such guardianship arrangements for minor children or the distribution of personal belongings or the appointment of executors. Consequently, even while nomination is a crucial part of estate planning, it should be used in concert with other legal documents like wills and trusts to guarantee thorough coverage and the execution of a person's last desires.

So What is the difference between Nomination and Will: ?

The legal notions of nomination and will are separate and have different functions in estate planning. The practice of naming beneficiaries for particular financial assets, including bank accounts, retirement accounts, or life insurance policies, is commonly referred to as nomination. By designating a beneficiary for an asset, a person effectively indicates to whom the asset's proceeds should be sent after their death. By using a simple nomination procedure, people can avoid the probate process and guarantee that their assets are transferred immediately to the designated recipients. But it's important to realize that a nomination by itself does not make a will.

A will, on the other hand, is a thorough legal document that specifies key issues including guardianship for young children, appointment of executors, and burial arrangements, as well as how a person's possessions and belongings should be dispersed after their death. A will, as contrast to a nomination, includes all of a person's assets, including those that are not susceptible to nomination, such real estate, personal property, and business interests. A will also gives people the freedom to define conditions on inheritances, make specific plans for the disposal of their estate, and handle other personal and family affairs. Nomination and will both are crucial to estate planning, but they have different functions and are best utilized in tandem to make sure that every part of a person's estate is taken care of and their last desires are carried out.

A nominee is nothing more than a trustee tasked with allocating the assets to the rightful heirs specified in a will or in accordance with local succession laws. For instance, a nominee receives the insurance payout upon the policyholder's death and then distributes it to the policyholder's legal heirs in accordance with the terms of the policyholder's will. On the other hand, individual succession laws apply when there is no will. When it comes to the Employee Provident Fund, things are much different. In this case, the beneficiary of the amount is the nominee rather than the individual named in the will. Unless you don't have any family at all, you are not allowed to designate anyone else to your EPF account than a family member, under EPF regulations. It is also possible to designate more than one family member and specify the percentage of the EPF that each would inherit.

Making a will is always recommended as part of the Retirement Planning, Financial Planning, and Wealth Management process. Building money or a corpus is only one facet of financial and retirement planning. Only when you have the final say over what happens to your accumulated corpus following your absence will your planning be considered complete. A wealth succession plan that outlines how your wealth will be distributed in accordance with your intentions is essential. It is only feasible if you leave a will that guarantees your spouse and kids receive your possessions.

What Does a Will Include ?

In a will, you can outline the allocation of your assets, including bank accounts, property, and valuables. If you own a business or investments, you can designate in your will exactly who receives what and when. You can also designate assets in your will to the charity or charities of your choice. Similarly, if you intend to leave property to a certain institution or group, a will helps ensure that your wishes are followed.

Not all of your possessions are protected by wills, even if the majority are. The testator's life insurance policy payments are one of the omitted items. The proceeds will be given to the beneficiaries specified in the policy. Similarly, this most likely applies to any investment accounts designated as "transfer on death." But there's a big catch: if the testator's beneficiaries outlived him or her, the policy or account reverts to the estate and gets divided as per the terms of the will or, if there isn't one, by the probate court, which is the part of the legal system that deals with wills, estates, and related matters.

Most states have regulations pertaining to elective shares or communal property that forbid disinheriting one's spouse. If a will leaves the surviving spouse with less of these assets than the state's required minimum—typically between 30% and 50%—a court may declare the will invalid. A will assigns guardianship of your minor children in the case of your death, in addition to allocating your possessions.

What Happens If I Die Without a Will ?

In the event that you die intestate—that is, without a will—the state distributes your assets, usually using a standard formula.

The above-mentioned elective-share and community property provisions mean that the formula often leaves your children with half of your estate and your spouse with half. The surviving spouse, who might have depended on the majority of your assets to maintain their level of living, would suffer if it became necessary to sell the family house or other assets under such circumstances.

If your children are minors, the court will designate a representative to represent their interests.

Dying intestate may also have fiscal implications because a well-drafted will can reduce estate taxes.

Getting started with Your Will

Make a list of your assets and debts to start drafting a will. Include any other assets you want to transfer to a particular person or entity, the contents of any safe deposit boxes, and any family heirlooms.

Make a list of the items you want to allocate to which heirs, if any, so that you can include it in your will later. Additionally, a letter of instruction, a separate document stored with the will, allows you to designate specific asset recipients. If this letter is the only thing you include assignments in, though, make sure your state will recognize them; some don't.

Compared to the will, the instruction letter can be written more casually. It might also contain details like account numbers, passwords, and even burial instructions that will help your executor deal with your estate. If a person becomes physically or mentally incapacitated, other will addenda, such as a power of attorney, a medical directive, or a living will, can specify how their affairs will be managed.

You might be tempted to make a single document that applies to both of you if you and your spouse struggle with willpower. resisted the urge. Estate planners almost universally advise against using joint wills, and some states don't even recognize them. Even if your will and your spouse's will end up looking eerily similar, having separate wills makes more sense.

How to Get Ready for and Validate Your Will

It's not always necessary to hire a lawyer to draught a valid will. Several software programs and DIY websites are available to help if you feel comfortable handling the task on your own. The document must be witnessed after you've finished it, typically by two adults who are familiar with you and of sound mind.

Any adult over the age of 18 who is deemed capable of doing so may serve as a witness to your will, but it's best to pick an impartial witness—someone who isn't a beneficiary and has no financial or emotional stake in your choices. In some states, you need two or more witnesses. Even though a lawyer can be a reliable witness, they shouldn't be if they also created the will.

Check the regulations in your state to see if a will needs to be notarized. You might want to have your witnesses fill out a self-proving affidavit even if that formality is not required. If the will is signed in front of a notary public, it may expedite the probate procedure by reducing the necessity of calling witnesses to testify in court to verify their signatures and the validity of the will.

Choosing Your Will's Executor

An executor of the estate who is still alive must be chosen. Typically, the executor of the estate is the spouse, adult child, or another dependable friend or family member. You can also name joint executors, such as your spouse or partner and your lawyer.

The probate court typically supervises the executor to make sure the directives in the will are carried out. You might want to appoint a lawyer or someone with legal and financial knowledge if your affairs are complicated.

You should retain legal counsel if your situation is complicated legally or your estate is sizable (in the millions of dollars). If this is the case, be sure to work with a will writer who is knowledgeable about the legal requirements in your state and has a wealth of experience in this area. Your state bar association might be able to help you find a qualified lawyer.

One of the most crucial things your will can do is to give your executor the authority to handle your finances and deal with debt collectors. Make sure your will's language permits this and gives your executor the power to manage related matters that aren't mentioned explicitly in your will.

Where should a Will be kept ?

A probate court typically needs to see your original will before it can handle your estate. Therefore, it is essential to store the document in a safe but accessible location. Avoid keeping it somewhere where your family might need a court order to access it, such as a bank safety deposit box. It is possible to have a home safe that is both waterproof and fireproof.

Then, at the very least, let your executor know where the original will is located and any other pertinent details, like the safe password. Additionally, create duplicate signed copies for the executor and your attorney, if necessary. The signed copies can be used to prove your intentions in the event that the original is lost or destroyed. On the other hand, if you don't have an original will, things may get complicated and there's no assurance that your estate will be distributed the way you'd like. Keep the document safe as a result.

How to change a Will

It's possible that you won't ever need to update your will. Additionally, you have the option of routinely updating it. Keep in mind that only the version of your will that is still in effect when you pass away counts.

A good general rule of thumb is to review your will every two to three years and during significant life transitions. Such events include things like marriage, divorce, and childbirth. Your children are unlikely to need guardians appointed in a will once they reach adulthood.

You can easily change your mind. To amend an existing will, you can either write a codicil or replace the existing will with a new one. Two witnesses are typically needed to sign a codicil because of how serious they are and how they have the power to alter the entire will, just as they were needed to sign the original will. Codicils are now permitted to be notarized in public notaries in some states, which have loosened the previously imposed legal restrictions on them.

Making any changes should ideally be done when you are in sound physical and mental health. As a result, there is a lower chance that your wishes will be successfully overturned and hasty or emotionally charged decisions are avoided.

A will offers your heirs a way to avoid conflict and potential taxes in addition to laying out where your assets should go. Examining your situation right away and creating the best will for you and your family can help any dependent children and keep you out of the probate court. No matter if you decide to do it yourself or work with an attorney, having a written will is prudent.

Epilogue

The process of planning for retirement is complex and calls for thoughtful analysis, wise judgment, and constant adjustment to shifting conditions. In this thorough examination of retirement preparation, we have covered a wide range of topics related to being emotionally, physically, and financially ready for life after work. Retirement planning includes a wide range of factors and obstacles, from setting goals and developing a savings plan to managing investments, reducing risks, and figuring out social security.

We've looked at how to create a sizable retirement fund by starting early, taking advantage of compound interest, and selecting wisely among your investments. We have also looked at how important risk management, asset allocation, and diversification are to safeguarding and increasing retirement assets over time. Furthermore, the function of individual retirement accounts (IRAs), employer-sponsored retirement plans, and other tax-advantaged savings vehicles in optimizing retirement savings and reducing tax obligations has been covered. We have also underlined the importance of periodically reviewing retirement plans, assumptions, and tactics in light of changing priorities, market conditions, and life events.

Retirement planning is a continuous process that calls for discipline, alertness, and flexibility to adjust to changing conditions and accomplish intended results. It is not a one-time event. Furthermore, we have emphasized how crucial it is to take into account non-financial elements including social ties, health care requirements, and lifestyle preferences in order to create a meaningful and rewarding retirement experience. Redefining one's purpose, priorities, and interests in life is a special chance that retirement brings, whether it is through travel, hobbies, volunteer work, or new professional options. We have also discussed the significance of wellness and health in retirement planning, including the necessity of having sufficient health insurance, long-term care planning, and techniques for preserving mental and physical health as we age.

We have also looked at the emotional aspects of retirement, such as the difficulties in making the shift from work to retirement, adjusting to identity and social network changes, and locating fulfillment and meaning in life after work. Retirement planning necessitates a thorough and all-encompassing approach to address all facets of the retirement journey, from creating a retirement income strategy to handling costs, taxes, and estate planning considerations. People can successfully negotiate the complexity of retirement planning by taking a proactive approach, getting expert advice, and remaining up to date on retirement trends and best practices.

Retirement planning is ultimately about creating a vision for the future, seizing new possibilities, and enjoying retirement to the fullest—it is about more than just financial security. People can attain their retirement goals and have a happy and successful retirement experience with careful planning, diligent saving, and wise decision-making.

Disclaimer

The information provided in this financial planning book is for educational and informational purposes only. It is not intended as financial, investment, tax, or legal advice. Readers are encouraged to seek professional advice from qualified financial advisors, accountants, or attorneys before making any financial decisions or implementing any strategies discussed in this book. The author and publisher disclaim any liability for the accuracy, completeness, or suitability of the information provided, and shall not be held responsible for any loss or damage resulting from reliance on the information contained herein. The views and opinions expressed in this book are those of the author and do not necessarily reflect the views of any affiliated organizations or institutions. Readers should exercise their own judgment and discretion when applying the concepts and principles discussed in this book to their individual financial situations. The content contains errors and omissions for which the author is not liable. There are no guarantees of completeness, accuracy, usefulness, or timeliness regarding the information on this website, which is provided "as is". We may not be able to accommodate every investor with our offerings of services and investments. You should consult an impartial financial advisor if you are unsure about the benefits of an investment.

Glossary

1) **Assets:** Assets are resources (currency, investments, real estate, and personal property) that belong to a person or organization and have a monetary worth.

2) **Liabilities:** A person's or an organization's outstanding debts or financial commitments, such as credit card debt, mortgages, and other liabilities.

3) **Net Worth:** Net worth is the total of a person's assets less their total obligations, which indicates their entire financial situation.

4) **Budgeting:** Making a plan for how income will be distributed to meet goals for savings and expenses within a given time period is known as budgeting.

5) **Savings:** Money put away for unexpected expenses or future needs; usually kept in certificates of deposit (CDs), savings accounts, or other liquid assets.

6) **Investments:** Investments are assets like stocks, bonds, mutual funds, real estate, and retirement accounts that are bought with the hope of earning income or appreciating in value over time.

7) **Risk Tolerance:** Risk tolerance is the capacity and willingness of an individual to accept changes in the value of their investments or the possibility of losing capital.

8) **Diversification:** Diversification of assets throughout several industries, geographical areas, and asset classes can help lower portfolio risk and volatility. This process is known as diversification.

9) **Asset allocation:** Asset allocation is the deliberate division of investments across several asset classes (e.g., cash, bonds, and equities) according to a person's time horizon, financial goals, and risk tolerance.

10) **Retirement Planning:** Retirement planning is the process of determining one's financial needs and devising a plan to invest money, save money, and earn a living after retirement.

11) **Compound interest:** Compound interest is interest that is earned on the principal amount as well as on interest that has accrued, which causes investments to grow exponentially over time.

12) **Inflation:** The overall rate of price increases for goods and services over time that devalues money and reduces buying power is known as inflation.

13) **Tax planning:** Tax planning is the use of credits, deductions, and investment vehicles like retirement accounts and tax-deferred savings plans to reduce tax obligations and maximize tax efficiency.

14) **Estate planning:** Estate planning, which frequently involves the use of wills, trusts, and other legal papers, is the process of making arrangements for the distribution of a person's assets and fortune to their heirs or beneficiaries following their death.

15) **Financial Goals:** Particular aims that people make in order to get their intended financial results, such debt repayment, house ownership, or retirement savings.

16) **Emergency fund:** An emergency fund is a savings account that is kept aside to deal with unforeseen costs or financial emergencies. It usually has three to six months' worth of living expenses in it.

17) **Credit score:** A person's credit score is a numerical assessment of their creditworthiness derived from their payment patterns, credit history, and general financial well-being.

18) **Financial Advisor:** A financial advisor is a specialist who offers direction and counsel on a range of personal finance topics, such as insurance, investments, retirement planning, and estate preparation.

19) **Risk management:** Risk management refers to techniques, such as insurance coverage and asset protection measures, to recognize, evaluate, and reduce any threats to a person's financial security and well-being.

20) **Financial literacy:** Financial literacy is the ability to make well-informed decisions on one's own finances and assets through knowledge and comprehension of financial concepts, principles, and practices.

About the Author

Dr. Sanjay Mittal has extensive expertise, a strong background in education, and is a Financial Analyst in addition to being a Senior Banker. He has six postgraduate degrees, fourteen certifications in Banking, Finance and Commerce including Advanced Financial Planning and an outstanding academic record. His greatest qualification is his Doctorate in Business Administration. He has extensive expertise in the BFSI and associated industries. He has extensive experience in Financial Planning and Wealth Management, Investment analysis and Banking management. He oversaw a sizeable group of financial experts and bankers. Financial Modeling, valuation methods, risk assessment, financial statement interpretation, technical and fundamental stock market analysis are among his strong suits. He is adept at assessing investment possibilities, portfolios and asset allocation plans. Dr. Sanjay is well versed in corporate finance, capital markets, mergers and acquisitions, loans and any other Banking Products and services.